THE GREAT GOLD COMEBACK

Bankruptcy of the Welfare State

by James R. Cook

Updated & Expanded
2021

190,000 copies in circulation

Print and design by By All Means Graphics
Project management by Alecia Schreckenberg

ISBN: 978-0-692-03566-5

TABLE OF CONTENTS

TABLE OF CONTENTS CONT.

ACKNOWLEDGMENTS

The first three chapters of this book are a rewrite of Donald Hoppe's 1972 book, *How To Invest in Gold Stocks and Avoid the Pitfalls*. When I began putting this volume together, I called Mr. Hoppe and asked if I could quote extensively from the first several chapters of his book. He suggested I rewrite it in my own words. Consequently I have condensed these three chapters, rewritten them and added additional facts.

I have taken the liberty to rewrite several paragraphs originally published by Ludwig von Mises. My purpose was to improve clarity and readability.

Many of the quotations in this book from authors and analysts have been condensed slightly for the sole purpose of improving readability.

INTRODUCTION

Not many things are worse than lying awake in the middle of the night racked with anxiety over financial losses. A panic, the inability to get a stock sold, illiquidity in a mutual fund, a bond fund that freezes redemptions, a mammoth drop in a favored stock, a margin call; these are terrifying events that cause suffering in the wee hours. The loss of retirement income, plunging asset values, mounting debts, reduced income and soaring losses are painful events that bring on the night terrors. Suffering over financial affairs can be every bit as painful as the anxiety that accompanies the wait for major surgery. Suffering is suffering.

If you have enough money to be comfortable for the balance of your life, now is the time to take measures to protect it from inflation. Whether your country is in a boom or a bust it's time to pin down your assets and secure them permanently. Some experts advise not to worry about it because the new paradigm makes bear markets, hyperinflation and depressions impossible. We don't believe that. When sound economic principles are cast to the wind, and excess become the norm, you must act independently. You need to own gold or silver as insurance against a severe financial loss.

When most everyone seems certain of a benevolent future and they are naïve of the pitfalls in stock investments that is a sign of trouble ahead. Lock up what you have. Don't believe that you can always get out before trouble hits. Any bubble could end with a panic. Liquidity could vanish. What are my credentials to be so certain? I have stuck with the gold business through almost 50 years of ups and downs. After a few decades it's just possible that I have learned something. I don't believe I have wasted my business life barking up the wrong tree. If I'm mistaken then so are a host of great economists, philosophers and thinkers. This book conveys the warnings of these experts.

A very real possibility exists that this nation could find itself in an untenable predicament that would force us into the equivalent of a national bankruptcy. America is not going to declare bankruptcy like a failing business does. However, if we have runaway inflation, a bond default or a dollar crash in foreign exchange markets it becomes similar to a bankruptcy. It's possible to end severe inflation by stopping the expansion of money and credit dead in its tracks, but that opens the door to a recession or worse. In effect, we are in between a rock and a hard place. Our government has to pay for a lot of what it spends through money printing which if continued long enough causes the money to lose its value. In that case it's inflate or die until the currency collapses and the people refuse to hold it. What we do after that is unknown. In the Weimar inflation the government simply issued a new currency. However, all the assets denominated in marks were lost.

Another subject we cover extensively in this book is the welfare predicament. The rising cost of subsidies contribute mightily to our budget deficits, money creation and inflation. Furthermore, the subsidized are afflicted with social problems that seem to worsen the longer they are on welfare. This growing underclass, with all its problems, represents a social predicament and a budgetary extravagance that can't be fixed or stopped short of a national bankruptcy.

It's hard for people to get a sense of the economic dangers and social perils we face. Every day government economists and Wall Street flacks assure us of a perpetual bull market. Consequently, most people have no fear. They cannot imagine hard times. They've never seen it, never thought about it. From millennials to the baby boomers, it's a lush life. Postponement of gratification doesn't fly. It's low savings and borrow to the hilt in this era of government safety nets and subsidies.

To own gold and silver you must have a sense of history. Easily created fiat money has invariably become worthless over time. There always have been panics, crashes, hyperinflations, disasters and depressions. During these events, a number of citizens suffer unbearable losses. Our record level of debt and spending has raised the possibility of the greatest monetary losses in history. When the financial system locks up, the liquidity doesn't exist for everyone to cash out painlessly. Gold insures against the stark punishment inherent in a financial earthquake. Get at least 10 to 20 percent of your total net worth into gold or silver coins or bars. Then hold them in your physical possession in a home safe or bank box. Someday they should secure you and protect you against the forces of runaway inflation and depression that can ravage the less insightful. In these high-flying days when markets are booming and worsening inflation waits in the wings, gold is a must.

CHAPTER I
GOLD AND CIVILIZATION

"The desire for gold is the most universal and deeply rooted commercial instinct of the human race."
~ Gerald M. Loeb

G old retains importance today but no longer influences history the way it once did. In the last century, governments reduced the monetary role of gold. Lenin scorned gold and promised to make bathroom fixtures with gold. Keynesian economists who influence U.S. economic policy consider it an unworkable relic. Gold ownership by U.S. citizens has fallen recently. This could change soon, and I believe gold will be restored to greater prominence than at any time in recent U.S. history. The decline of the dollar and worsening inflation will set in motion another comeback for gold and launch a renewed age of influence for the yellow metal. Furthermore, aggressive buying by Asians and Europeans supports the price.

Gold has always occupied an important place in human affairs. Nations flourished with gold as money and entire cultures died off without it. The wealth and power of ancient Persia can be linked to the Persian gold coin, the daric. Their gold money brought them commercial success. When Alexander the Great conquered the Persians, he used the gold he captured to further his military objectives.

Early civilizations that relied on gold achieved great success. The Byzantine Empire lasted for 800 years based on its gold coin, the bezant. It was no coincidence that shortly after eliminating gold coinage, the Byzantine Empire disappeared. The economy of ancient Rome was reduced to a shambles once they debased the purity and value of their coinage. The great Spanish empire rose and fell with the amount of gold they extracted from the Americas.

The history of gold serves as a road map to the progress of civilization. Gold money fuels commerce and sparks those rare but important bursts of progress that highlight the ages. Valuable historical artifacts made of gold testify to gold's role as the supreme metal of the arts. It continues to this day to be an industrial commodity and high fashion adornment of great value.

Since gold is easily worked, jewelers and artisans prize the lustrous yellow metal. Gold remains unaffected by water or oxygen. It neither rusts nor corrodes. Unlike silver, gold does not tarnish. It is virtually imperishable and one of the most stable elements. Its density and softness afford it a wealth of uses. An ounce of gold can be stretched into a wire 50 miles long. It can be pounded into a flat sheet as big as a house. It can plate a copper wire for 1,000 miles. Gold conducts electricity so well that a microscopic amount can replace miles of wiring inside a computer. If it were cheaper in price its uses would multiply beyond measure.

Even before gold was used as money, it was considered as the ultimate form of wealth for kings, merchants and the early Church. Gold was the first substance mentioned in the Bible. Gold artifacts and jewelry have been found that date back 6,000 years. Fabulous gold treasures were found in the tomb of King Tut. The Pharaoh's body was encased in a coffin made from 25,000 ounces of solid gold.

Nothing else in history served to display wealth, power and prestige as did gold jewelry and gold artifacts that were the epitome of early art and craftsmanship.

The great archaeologist Heinrich Schliemann made enough money in the California gold rush to help finance his excavation of Troy and Mycenae. After discovering a golden death mask he wired authorities, "I have looked upon the face of Agamemnon." The golden treasures he dug up at Troy were housed in a Berlin museum and removed in 1945 by the Russians. They were thought to have been melted into bars, but in 1994 some of the treasure was found in Russian museums.

Among early civilizations, gold evolved into a prized possession. Beauty and scarcity enhanced mankind's desire for it. A tiny amount of gold took on a high value. Great wealth could now be safely stored in a small hiding place. It could be buried and not rot. It was impervious to moisture and dampness. These factors were instrumental in the transforming of gold from an item of value into the role of money.

Prior to the evolution of money, barter was the primary means of negotiating a transaction. An exchange of cattle for grain or weapons could prove cumbersome. A medium of exchange that stored value and acted as a unit of account could make commercial life far easier.

Money has been everything from sea shells to beads. In modern times cigarettes and chocolate have temporarily served as money. Gold stood out. No one turned down gold. No one could get enough of it. Nothing else provided the deep-seated psychological satisfaction of gold. Furthermore, the yellow metal could be broken into small units, each having a high value. It was durable and portable. More than any other form of money, gold built confidence. It established a solid underpinning for trade and commerce. When gold first began to serve as money, it must surely have been responsible for a great boom in commercial activity and was thus a principal engine of human progress.

About 2,000 years before Christ, the early Babylonians developed a system of weights and measures that added greatly to the ability of gold to serve as money. The Babylonian shekel, a small gold bar, became the common monetary unit. The shekel enabled the Babylonians to dominate commercial activity in the Fertile Crescent (modern Iraq) and build an important early culture. While it was the Babylonians who created gold bars, it was a small, short-lived kingdom (in what is now Turkey) that invented coinage. This was Lydia, the country of the legendary monarch, Croesus. In approximately 55 BC, Lydia struck the first gold coins. These crude lumps of pure gold were quickly imitated by the Greeks, who were soon to strike the first silver coins. The use of coins expanded rapidly from the Mediterranean to the Mideast. The Greeks elevated the engraving and minting of coins to a high art form.

The Romans never seemed to get the hang of stable money. They were the first major inflators in history. Rome constantly experimented with clipping or debasing its coinage. The Romans tried to engineer a form of money that could be debased without a corresponding loss of value. They watered down the purity of their coinage but strived to keep the purchasing power intact. Sounds familiar doesn't it?

One exception was Julius Caesar, who upon taking control of the Roman Republic, introduced a gold standard. His coinage, the aureus, brought on a period of financial calm that lasted almost a century. Subsequent emperors, however, diluted the coinage once again. It did not occur to the Romans that a sound and honorable monetary unit could keep their empire together through means other than force. Inflation, as much as any other factor, contributed to the downfall of the Roman Empire. Historians often draw comparisons between Rome and modern day currency debasement.

CHAPTER II

GOLD AND WESTERN EUROPE

"Gold was not selected arbitrarily by governments to be the monetary standard. Gold had developed for many centuries on the free market as the best money; as the commodity providing the most stable and desirable monetary medium."

~ Murray N. Rothbard

Prosperity and progress flourished with the widespread monetary use of gold. The stability of gold money brought about dramatic commercial and cultural advancements. Social and political upheavals have been rare under a gold standard. Sustained economic progress seems to require gold coinage or gold-backed money.

The emergence of the Italian city-states in the 13th century led to a period of enlightenment and a rich cultural renaissance. Human progress had come to a standstill during six centuries of the dark ages. At first Florence, and then Venice, issued gold coins. There followed a period of prosperity that pulled Western Europe out of the doldrums.

Unfortunately in the centuries that followed, the monarchs and rulers of England and the continent developed a fondness for clipping and debasing their coins. This pilferage worked much better than the alchemists who promised to transmute base metals into gold. Centuries of chronic debasement from dishonest rulers contributed to the economic stagnation of feudalism.

The influx of gold into Spain from the New World was at the heart of a burst of economic activity that swept through Europe in the 16th century. Spain flourished, its timeless art and literature personified by Velásquez and Cervantes. Once the gold stopped flowing out of Mexico and South America, Spain declined as rapidly as it had vaulted to prominence.

No matter how much gold had been funneled into Spain, there was always a cry for more. Throughout history complaints about the scarcity of money have been commonplace. Cures for this shortage are invariably schemes to dilute the existing money stock, despite the fact that creating more money cannot by itself increase the wealth of the people. Gold meets the most stringent definitions of liquid wealth, and this pure form of money can only be produced through an elaborate mining process. In fact, a slow increase in gold money through mining seems vastly preferable to the printing press method of money creation, since the former has a natural brake on expansion, while the latter has no such safeguard.

The view that more and more money must be made available in order to expand the economy is a myth. It's in a recession or depression that the cry for new money becomes loudest. But the unbridled expansion of money creates an unhealthy boom in the first place. The liquidation of the excesses of the boom leads to a bust. If the money supply remains stable, as with gold, then increased production will cause prices for goods to drop. That's just one of the many benefits of sound money, in contrast to the inflationary tricks of modern government.

Paper money made its appearance slightly over 300 years ago. This early money was a receipt from a goldsmith who kept a safe storage place for gold. These receipts came to be circulated widely as a method of payment. The U.S. government used similar gold certificates in the 19th and early 20th centuries, redeemable in gold owned by the government.

At the beginning of the 17th century, banks began to experiment with the issuance of bank credit as a means of payment. Governments rapidly latched on to this practice of creating fiat money as a way to pay off their debt. In 18th-century France this resulted in two of the worst hyper-inflations in history. These hyper-inflations led to the French Revolution, a period of political, social and financial chaos which enabled Napoleon Bonaparte to take power. Sometimes, periods of monetary upheaval bring a dictatorship.

Major gold discoveries by the '49ers in California soon made enough of the yellow metal available to put the world on a gold standard.

With money creation out of the hands of the politicians, the industrial revolution gave birth to our modern era. Enough gold was mined in Alaska, the Yukon and in South Africa by the end of the 19th century, to make gold coinage widespread throughout the world. This period of great economic growth dramatically increased living standards for millions of Americans, attracting a steady influx of immigrants to share in the wealth and opportunity of capitalism. In terms of productivity, enhanced living conditions (starvation eliminated and pestilence controlled), no period in history can compare with that time in which America lived under the gold standard. Economic growth catapulted forward with dynamic increases year after year.

Unfortunately, governments the world over invariably abolished the discipline of gold when emergencies arose. It is a measure of the corruption of modern governments how often they resort to currency debasement.

Loose money and credit policies financed the futility and waste of the First World War and led to a breakdown of the gold standard. The Germans, who were left destitute by the war, experimented with fiat money and introduced one of the great hyper-inflations in history. Large quantities of paper currency were issued in Germany throughout the early 1920's, eventually driving daily price levels to astronomical levels. A German woman supposedly wheeled a baby buggy full of money to her local bakery to buy a loaf of bread. She left it outside for a moment while she went in to the bakery. When she came out, someone had dumped the money onto the street and had stolen the buggy.

The destructive German inflation sowed the seeds of national discord that proved fertile ground for the National Socialists and Hitler. So often in history, a period of monetary chaos enables an extremist to take power. After the Second World War in China the Nationalists fought to stay in control while inflation raged. They paid their army with paper money. Mao Tse Tung paid his army with silver coins. Ultimately, his Red Army evicted the Nationalists from China and they fled to Formosa (Taiwan). Those citizens who had paper money couldn't get out of the country. Those who had gold were able to buy passage out when the Red Army rolled across China.

CHAPTER III
GOLD IN AMERICA

"For more than two thousand years gold's natural qualities made it man's universal medium of exchange. In contrast to political money, gold is honest money that survived the ages and will live on long after the political fiats of today have gone the way of all paper."

~ Hans. F. Sennholz

In colonial America, gold coins were scarce. Early colonists relied on beaver pelts, tobacco, musket balls, gun powder and rum for money and barter. The principal silver coin was the Spanish silver dollar. The colonists cut the Spanish dollar into halves and quarters to make smaller denominations. From this practice came the terms "two bits" and "four bits."

The Revolutionary War forced our poor nation to issue the Continental dollar, a paper currency unbacked by gold. After the war these Continental dollars soon became worthless. The new Constitution mandated production of silver dollars and gold coins in denominations of 2½ dollars, 5 dollars and 10 dollars. The first U.S. Mint located in Philadelphia began stamping out this gold coinage in 1792. Early gold discoveries in California provided an ample supply of gold in America and fostered a de facto gold standard. Although the gold standard became an official government act in 1900, the United States had in reality been on a gold standard since 1830.

Economist Hans Sennholz (1922-2007) stated, "The gold standard is as old as civilization." Throughout the ages, the gold standard emerged again and again because man needed a dependable medium of exchange. Gold provided such a medium. It was the most marketable good that gradually gained universal employment and thus became money. Its natural qualities, its use for the manufacture of ornaments and jewelry, its easy divisibility, great durability, storability and transportability, made this precious metal well suited to serve as money.

The leading economist of the Austrian School of economics Ludwig von Mises (1881-1973) wrote, "The gold standard has one tremendous virtue: the quantity of the money supply, under the gold standard, is independent of the policies of governments and political parties. This is its advantage. It is a form of protection against spendthrift governments."

Mises claimed, "The gold standard was the world standard of the age of capitalism, increasing welfare, liberty, and democracy, both political and economic…. It was the medium of exchange by means of which Western industrialism and Western capital had borne Western civilization into the remotest parts of the earth's surface, everywhere destroying the fetters of age-old prejudices and superstitions, sowing the seeds of new life and new well-being, freeing minds and souls, and creating riches unheard of before."

The United States began divorcing itself from the gold standard during the Great Depression. Credit expansion throughout the 1920s made it impossible to redeem these newly created dollars for gold. The gold reserves were not large enough. The stock market crash, bank failures and bankruptcies created a demand for gold. Panic and fear caused depositors to withdraw gold and currency to the point that there were runs on many banks. Rather than massively devalue the dollar to maintain gold convertibility, the newly elected Roosevelt administration declared a bank holiday.

This emergency order was followed a few days later by an executive order to all citizens demanding the surrender of all gold coins, gold bullion and gold certificates to the Federal Reserve within 25 days. Failure to comply was punishable by 10 years in prison and a large fine. The game plan was to stabilize the dollar in world exchange markets. The seizure of gold gave the government large enough reserves to retain international convertibility. Foreign governments could convert dollars into the gold, but U.S. citizens could not. Roosevelt hoped that this would make the dollar sound. Ultimately (40 years later), even foreign governments were denied this convertibility.

After World War II the economic philosophy of John Maynard Keynes prevailed in Western Europe. Since Keynesians had little use for gold they saw that it was divorced from money. This policy helped lead to widespread money creation and inflation. Subsequently, over the past 60 years, the dollar has lost more than 90% of its purchasing power.

The brilliant economist Murray Rothbard (1926-1995) wrote: "For a half-century, the Keynesians have harbored a dream. They have long dreamed of a world without gold, a world rid of any restrictions upon their desire to spend and spend, inflate and inflate, elect and elect. They have achieved a world where governments and central banks are free to inflate without suffering the limits and restrictions of the gold standard. But they still chafe at the fact that, although national governments are free to inflate and print money, they yet find themselves limited by depreciation of their currency. What the Keynesians want is no less than an internationally coordinated and controlled world-wide, paper-money inflation, a fine-tuned inflation that would proceed unchecked upon its merry way until, whoops! It landed the entire world smack into the middle of the untold horrors of global runaway hyperinflation."

When the international gold standard was abolished, it was replaced by a paper standard. Variations of the paper standard exist today and have allowed the United States to run large deficits. Mises argued, "The gold standard did not collapse. Governments abolished it in order to pave the way for inflation." Analyst Graham Summers tells us, "Once the U.S. abandoned the gold standard completely in 1971, the amount of debt in the U.S. financial system skyrocketed relative to the real economy. As a result of this, by the time the mid-1990s rolled around, debt levels in the U.S. financial system had become a systemic risk: with this much leverage in the system, even a brief bout of debt deflation would induce a systemic crisis. Consider that the Great Financial Crisis of 2008, the one during which everyone thought the world was ending, caused the Federal Reserve to intentionally create bubbles in various asset classes in order to keep the financial system solvent. There's one big problem with this however. Asset bubbles always burst, triggering crises."

In his book *Beyond Our Means*, former Wall Street Journal editor, Alfred A. Malabre, Jr. wrote, "Our willingness, even determination to live beyond our means – to go far more deeply into debt than our resources safely will allow – has led to ominous patterns…. If America sinks deeper and deeper into debtor-nation status, painful bills will begin coming due. Americans will be compelled to give up more and more of their income simply to pay interest to creditors."

The United States has managed year after year to run up astonishing budget and trade deficits with only minimal damage to the dollar in foreign exchange markets. How long foreigners will, or can continue to swallow $1 trillion of our money or more each year is an open question. This process cannot be sustained indefinitely. The threat to the value of the dollar can't be overstated. When the dollar plunge begins in earnest, gold will tend to directly offset this loss.

According to economist Kurt Richebächer, "The yawning gap in foreign trade and the U.S. economy's foreign indebtedness are now of such stupendous proportions that any comparisons with the past or any attempt to quantify the ultimate impact of the bursting of this bubble appear extremely hazardous. But it's safe to say that with their potential adverse effects on the dollar, the trade deficit and the accumulating foreign indebtedness are the paramount threats to the stability of the whole U.S. economy with immeasurable implications for the world."

The economist John Williams tells us, "Unless the United States addresses the long-range solvency issues currently in play for the U.S. Treasury, a hyperinflation will hit the United States, and it likely will be set off much earlier than most anticipate, by any number of factors that could trigger a panicked sell-off in the U.S. dollar. The current tightening in monetary policy threatens to damage major sectors of U.S. economic activity. Such an intensifying economic downturn would stress banking-system liquidity. The U.S. central bank's primary concern remains the maintenance of solvency and liquidity in a still troubled banking system. Intensifying economic and financial stresses remain likely to cause the (Federal Open Market Committee) FOMC to back off its current pattern of rate hikes and balance-sheet liquidation, to revert towards expanded quantitative easing.... Holding physical gold and silver remain the ultimate hedges – stores of wealth – for preserving the purchasing power of one's U.S. dollar assets, in the context of liquidity and portability, during the difficult and highly inflationary times that lie ahead."

Gold expert Egon von Greyerz claims, "Gold will continue to be the only currency to survive in history just as it has for almost 5,000 years. Physical gold and silver are the ultimate forms of wealth preservation as well as insurance against the economic and financial calamities that the world will experience in coming years."

The lack of interest in gold on the part of the American public at such a critical juncture in the history of our currency should appeal to all contrary-opinion investors. At perhaps the most critical time in U.S. history, gold bores the financial experts and mystifies the public.

Furthermore gold is seldom, if ever, given much thought in government circles. The U.S. gold reserves are never mentioned in Washington affairs. Politicians have little or no understanding of the role of gold. Years ago, a U.S. Senator suggested that our gold reserves be sold off to depress gold prices and punish South Africa. He gave up the idea because low gold prices would also harm U.S. gold mining companies. He was ignorant of the fact that U.S. gold reserves are part of the national patrimony and still act as a de facto reserve behind the dollar.

In a monetary crisis, foreigners and investors who hold dollars may consider how many ounces of gold stand behind the U.S. dollar. If our government ever sells off the U.S. gold reserve it could mean that the dollar would plunge further and lose its role as the world's reserve currency. Once the dollar loses its value through devaluation or hyper-inflation, any new currency would need this gold for convertibility, or it would fare no better than the ruined currency it replaces.

Analyst Brandon Smith writes, "Trillions of dollars in uncontrolled central bank stimulus and years of artificially low interest rates have poisoned every aspect of our financial system. Nothing functions as it used to. In fact, many markets actually move in the exact opposite manner as they did before the debt crisis began in 2008. The most obvious example has been stocks, which have enjoyed the most historic bull market ever despite all fundamental data being contrary to a healthy economy. All hell's about to break loose."

CHAPTER IV

GOLD TO THE PRESENT

*"Gold would have value if for no other reason than it enables
a citizen to fashion his financial escape from the state."*

~ William F. Rickenbacker

Fiat money dovetailed nicely with the prevalent political philosophy that gained influence in the U.S. after the Second World War. Building on the initiatives of the Roosevelt administration, the government aimed to take an even greater role in solving national problems and regulating the economy. Thus sprang up our social welfare policy and the promise of a guaranteed life. This something-for-nothing philosophy grew into a wide range of government entitlements. From the beginning, this policy led to excessive government spending, which continues to worsen to this day.

In the 1960's government spending began to run away. Although political candidates promised to balance the budget and cut programs, none ever did. As the government spent more than it brought in through taxes, it began to borrow heavily in the capital markets. Over several decades, the budget deficit grew to annual amounts that were impossible to comprehend. The national debt (the accumulation of yearly deficits) soared into the trillions of dollars.

Meanwhile, the U.S. central bank, the Federal Reserve, intermittently launched vast expansions in the money supply to cure periodic economic slumps and to help finance or liquidate the government's debt. This led to severe rounds of price inflation that eroded the value of the dollar.

Alarmed about the damaging monetary trends that were unfolding in the 1960's, the economist Henry Hazlitt wrote in an October, 1963, issue of Newsweek, "The basic assumption of all governments today is that they not only have the right but the duty to tamper constantly with the national money. This is known as monetary management. They reject the only real solution (to sound money) – a return to a full international gold standard. They repeat the old charge that this was the system which broke down after WWI and led to the currency chaos of the '30s. The gold standard did not break down; it was deliberately abandoned and destroyed by monetary managers who wanted to dilute and inflate their national currencies, and who rightly recognized the gold standard as the great barrier to their plans. The reason governments are now opposed to a return to the full gold standard is that it would deprive them of their present powers to manage and expand – in brief, to inflate."

Inflation led to a renewed interest in gold. In 1968, the gold price broke loose from its fixed rate of $35 and rose to $44. In the early 1970's gold broke out again, rising to $65 an ounce in the spring of 1972. When gold ownership was once again legalized on January 1, 1975, gold touched the $200 an ounce mark. (Gold legalization was not all that it was cracked up to be. Americans had been vigorously buying gold coins for years that were restrikes of early coins, while the government winked at this loophole.)

Sparked by a wave of double-digit inflation in 1979-1980, gold prices soared to record levels. In February, of 1980, in a frenzy of trading activity, gold reached $850 per ounce. This price peak capped a multi-year rise that pushed gold into the investment limelight as never before. A steep decline in silver prices broke the back of the precious metals market as the government put a nasty squeeze on the Hunt brothers, who had invested heavily in silver. Inflation abated and gold prices fell off. Gold established a trading pattern throughout the balance of the 1980s between $250 and $500.

Gold prices have reacted favorably to dollar declines and to price inflation. In the early part of the 1990s gold held up reasonably well in a recession. In 1993, gold prices started up again, reached $400 and then returned to $300 in 1998. For the next five years gold moved hardly at all. In 2004, it reached $454 and ran up each year thereafter until 2011 when it reached $1,895 an ounce. In the years that followed it settled between $1,200 and $1,300. Recent predictions from gold experts suggest it will reach new highs.

For the future, gold should react favorably in a stock market crash or in a deflationary panic when illiquid assets are dumped on the market. Unquestionably, gold would perform well if high inflation dilutes the dollar's purchasing power, or when foreign exchange markets weaken the value of the dollar against other currencies. Gold guru Frank Holmes writes, "A weaker U.S. dollar, a steadily flattening yield curve, heightened market volatility, overvalued U.S. stocks, expectations of higher inflation, trade war jitters, geopolitical risks and more makes the investment case for gold more compelling than at any other time in recent memory."

Author Simon Black writes about the availability of gold in the future: "It takes nature hundreds of millions of years to deposit minerals deep in the earth's crust while human beings only require a few decades to pull most of it out. This creates the constant need for mining companies to explore for more and more major discoveries. Problem is – that's not happening. Mining companies aren't finding any more vast deposits. According to Pierre Lassonde, founder of the gold royalty giant Franco-Nevada and former head of Newmont Mining – If you look back to the 70s, 80s and 90s, in every one of those decades, the industry found at least one 50+ million-ounce gold deposit, at least ten 30+ million-ounce deposits, and countless 5- to 10-million-ounce deposits. But if you look at the last 15 years, we found no 50-million-ounce deposit, no 30-million-ounce deposit and only very few 15-million-ounce deposits. So where are those great big deposits we found in the past? How are they going to be replaced? We don't know.

"The deep concern that inflation is coming (or has already arrived) is completely valid. Inflation is a huge problem. And the traditional hedge in times of inflation is gold. But remember – new gold discoveries have collapsed in the past 15 years. And, as Lassonde said, there are few discoveries on the horizon to make up the difference. These companies can't just go out and start a new mine, either. Even if they found a promising deposit, with all of the bureaucratic red tape, it would take seven to nine years to start producing gold. So when demand for gold really starts to heat up, the supply won't be there. And this could really cause the gold price to soar."

The thing to remember about gold is that it was always the world's money until government grew into a dominant force and gave gold the boot. This happened in the early part of the last century when gold money was replaced by paper money. Today many would say that gold is no longer money. It's no longer a unit of account or a medium of exchange, and its importance as a store of value has lessened. No doubt about it, gold is temporarily on the sidelines as money. That's primarily because when gold is money it won't let governments inflate or expand credit. It's simple to increase the quantity of paper money, you merely print it. Gold has to be dug from the ground.

But what if paper money were to fail? Gold would be money again. It's good to look at gold as a back-up money. It's the money that always emerges when paper money fails. Paper money has this terrible flaw that it can be created endlessly out of thin air. Whereas gold has this tremendous virtue that it can't be. If you think of gold as an alternative money that is biding time while the government and Wall Street fiddle with paper money in order to feather their own nest, you will get to the nub of it. Gold is the ultimate hedge against the failure of the government's money. Ray Dalio the founder of Bridgewater Associates, the world's biggest hedge fund recently said, "If you don't have 5% to 10% of your assets in gold as a hedge, we'd suggest you relook at this."

Author Gary Christenson sums it up: "The United States' fiscal and monetary policies passed 'crazy' long ago, and now are pushing deeper into insanity with out-of-touch Federal Reserve policy, insane debt, uncontrolled deficit spending, and a 'what could go wrong' attitude. Clearly the 'paper game' has a limited life expectancy, Wall Street is due for a reset, government spending programs and pension plans are on life support, food stamps and student loans are two of many programs aggressively pushing the U.S. government into insolvency. Bubbles always pop. Delusions can persist for years or decades, but they eventually crash on the rocky shores of reality. Gold and silver were valuable 3,000 years before the first central bank and I submit they will be valuable 3,000 years after the world regains monetary sanity. Given the endless borrow-and-spend programs, ever increasing debt, and overpriced stocks and bonds, have you stocked physical gold in preparation for the inevitable consequences of all the above?"

CHAPTER V
THE SPENDING PROBLEM

"Even during the period when Rome lost much of her ancient prestige, an Indian traveler observed that trade all over the world was operated with the aid of Roman gold coins which were accepted and admired everywhere."

~ Paul Einzig

Government spending is built in and uncontrollable. This runaway spending is the root cause of the chronic inflation that lurks in the wings. Ultimately, it can wreck the dollar, impair the economy, and reduce our living standards. It will make us poorer rather than wealthier. Nobody in America seems all that worried about $28 trillion in debt. But they should be. It's the reason you need to have silver and gold. A big jump in interest rates could ruin us. Bond selling by foreigners could spark runaway inflation. A decline in foreign demand for dollars could sink our currency and destroy the bond market. We're sitting on a powder keg attached to a burning fuse.

Author Stefan Gleason wrote, "The Congressional Budget Office projects that publicly held federal debt as a percentage of the economy will soon surge past all previous wartime spikes. The official national debt of nearly $28 trillion is just the tip of the iceberg. It represents a small proportion of the total unfunded liabilities the political class has racked up over the past few decades. Taxpayers are on the hook for perhaps $100 trillion more in unfunded entitlement and pension IOUs. Trillions upon trillions of dollars have been promised that simply won't exist…unless the Federal Reserve creates them out of nothing. The Fed's unlimited power to expand the currency supply enables politicians to commit acts of fiscal malfeasance with political impunity."

Analyst Kevin Muir explains the dimensions of the problem: "We all know the terrifying debt statistics. We are bombarded every day with bearish reports about the gargantuan federal debt, and when combined with the growing private sector indebtedness, the monolithic entitlements problem, and the looming pension fund shortage, it is easy to wonder how we will ever get out of this colossal mess. Given the enormous debt problem, the notion we will pay it back in real terms through growth, or even more improbably, the idea of allowing a massive debt destruction event to reset the system, is unrealistic. Any economic weakness will be met with more printing, and more stimulus. Maybe governments allow one or two quarters of weakness. It might even drag on for a year. But then as sure as day follows night, they will inflate again. They simply cannot afford not to. What happens when economic growth picks up and causes inflation? Given the massive indebtedness, central banks will be loath to raise rates enough to cool inflation. This will only cause more inflation. Eventually we will hit a point where governments will be unable to raise rates because it would crush their balance sheets, yet inflation will dictate rates be higher. This will be checkmate. Governments will have no moves. Inflation will soar, the yield curve will steepen (to record-wide), and the inflationary reset will be upon us."

Author Danielle DiMartino Booth writes, "We have gone from $150 trillion (in global debt) in 2007 to $220 trillion and counting today. If you delude yourself into thinking a rising rate environment can be good when we have tacked on $70 trillion of debt in the last decade, you are fooling yourself. It is an accident waiting to happen, and anyone who doesn't think that it will take the stock market down with it is more optimistic than I am by a country mile. Figure out a way to have exposure to precious metals."

The government does not cut expenses when revenues decline as does private business. Rather, their built-in costs rise as various programs are called upon by those who find their economic conditions worsening. At the same time they must service trillions in debt with the possibility of interest rates pushing higher. A bad outcome is inevitable. No country can spend recklessly on expensive social welfare schemes and in the face of an unprecedented debt bubble keep on spending. No country can subsidize rich and poor until half its population gets a government check. No country can do all this and still have the world's biggest military, fight expensive wars and stick its nose into other countries' business. It's not going to work. The train is leaving the station. The U.S. has cooked its goose. A sorry outcome is likely. The only question is when? Our finances are in a shambles yet we persist in spending far more than we have. We borrow half of the money needed to finance our extravagances. Our politicians and bureaucrats continue to add costly programs. Our monetary authorities print up the money that we can't borrow. This excess can ultimately plunge us into despair.

This country is in the grip of a falsehood that has risen to dominate the culture; the belief that big government is our savior. Our economists and our educators promote a radical dogma. Our media spreads the phony Keynesian doctrine of easy money. We are at $21 trillion and counting on the road to perdition. The big-spending progressive agenda is the blueprint for national ruin. Someday soon the bond vigilantes will arrive. Our bankruptcy is probably cooked in the books. What's left unsaid is that this winding path of excess and extravagance that we are following is more than just a road to national insolvency. It is the certain path to the dismantling of everything that has made America great.

Frequently the cry arises to cut government waste and make the bureaucracy more efficient. That won't work. Government doesn't have a bottom line. Unlike private enterprise, which measures results by profit or loss, government has no such yardstick. Government officials measure results by how much money they spend. That's why they always lobby for more money. *Government has no objective means to measure results.* There is no incentive for cost cutting or sound financial management.

Government seldom relies on merit as does business. They tend to measure employees by credentials and educational degrees. Merit often takes a back seat to political motives and to not rocking the boat. Private enterprise must constantly struggle to become more cost effective. That's why business pays close attention to the work ethic and to the merit of employees. By some estimates, private business is five to ten times more efficient than government.

When government redistributes as much money as it does, the nation becomes a hotbed of politics. Special interest groups elbow up to the government trough. Lobbyists maneuver to cash in on the bounty in Washington. Politicians and bureaucrats who control the purse strings become media stars. Payola and corruption rise and politics flourish. The beneficiaries of the social welfare system and the other recipients of government spending will fight to the bitter end to maintain these privileges. The numbers of the subsidized have become so large and influential that they can elect politicians that demand corporations and the affluent be bled dry. The leftists they elect will gladly oblige this demand. The government bureaucracy never can be reformed or made efficient. Don't look to them to reduce our spending and debts.

Editor Michael Snyder sums it up, "We are living during the greatest debt bubble in the history of the world, and our financial engineers have got to keep figuring out ways to keep it growing much faster than global GDP because if it ever stops growing it will burst and destroy the entire global financial system. Bill Gross, a respected financial mind, recently observed that 'our highly levered financial system is like a truckload of nitroglycerin on a bumpy road.' And he is precisely correct. Everything might seem fine for a while, but one day we are going to hit the wrong bump at the wrong time and the whole thing is going to go ka-boom.

"The financial crisis of 2008 represented an opportunity to learn from our mistakes, but instead we just papered over our errors and cranked up the global debt creation machine to levels never seen before. According to the International Monetary Fund, global debt has grown to a staggering grand total of 281 trillion dollars. Other estimates put that figure closer to 300 trillion dollars. When you go into debt there are consequences. And when the greatest debt bubble in human history finally bursts, the consequences will be exceedingly severe. The best that our leaders can do for now is to keep the bubble alive for as long as possible, because what comes after the bubble is gone will be absolutely unthinkable."

The outcome of runaway social welfare and runaway government spending may lead inevitably to the destruction of the dollar and a soaring price for gold.

CHAPTER VI
THE ECONOMIST

"In the long run, the gold price has to go up in relation to paper money. There is no other way. To what price, that depends on the scale of the inflation – and we know that inflation will continue."

~ Nicholas L. Deák

Ludwig von Mises (1881-1973) (pronounced Meesez) was born in the Austro-Hungarian Empire. Hard money advocates and free market economists consider him to be the greatest economic thinker in history. He believed in limited government, the gold standard, sound money, capitalism and personal freedom. If you have never heard of him, it's time you learned more. Mises attended the University of Vienna during the high tide of the "Austrian School" of economics. His accomplishments are prodigious. In 1920, he showed that socialism and planning must fail because of the lack of market pricing. Mises' insightful checkmate to collectivism was widely acknowledged years later when communism collapsed.

Among other things, Mises was able to show that inflation was no more than taxation and redistribution of wealth; that prices will most often fall without government-induced money injections; that increases in the money supply, e.g. a sudden doubling of everyone's money-holding benefits society not an iota and in fact only dilutes purchasing power; that only growth in the factors of production, land, labor, plant and equipment will increase production and standards of living.

In a brilliant and important theoretical accomplishment Mises answered a problem most economists thought unanswerable. How can we explain that the price of money is influenced by demand if to have demand it must first have a price? He traced the time component in the demand for money back in time to a useful barter commodity (e.g. silver and gold). The dramatic implications meant money could only originate on the free market out of demand. Government, despite any attempts to the contrary, could not originate money. Money is not arbitrary pieces of paper but must originate as a useful and valuable commodity.

Mises also pointed out how central banking acts as an accomplice to government money expansion. And he began to explain his great business cycle theory. Recognizing that the market economy could not generate by itself a series of booms and busts he fixed the blame on an outside factor – the habitual expansion of money and credit. He argued that a credit-induced boom must eventually "lead to a crack-up boom." He wrote, "The boom can last only as long as the credit expansion progresses at an ever-accelerated pace. The boom comes to an end as soon as additional quantities of fiduciary media are no longer thrown upon the loan market. But it could not last forever even if inflation and credit expansion were to go on endlessly. It would then encounter the barriers which prevent the boundless expansion of circulation credit. It would lead to the crack-up boom and the breakdown of the whole monetary system."

He warned, "The credit expansion boom is built on the sands of banknotes and deposits. It must collapse." He stated, "If the credit expansion is not stopped in time, the boom turns into the crack-up boom; the flight into real values begins, and the whole monetary system founders. Continuous inflation (credit expansion) must finally end in the crack-up boom and the complete breakdown of the currency system." Mises further claimed that, "Expansion (of credit) squanders scarce factors of production by malinvestment and overconsumption." Malinvestment means building too many shopping centers and not enough factories. Overconsumption means a borrowing-and-spending boom by consumers that depletes savings and reduces capital investment.

Mises was aware that a credit excess could spill over into stock and bond speculation. But even he would be surprised at today's unprecedented level of credit-induced speculation. He would be depressed by the astonishing levels of public and private debt, government borrowing, central bank market interventions, trade deficits, non-bank credit growth, money velocity, illiquidity, the manipulation of interest rates and foreign indebtedness. The magnitude of these excesses seemingly without penalties would appear to be rewriting the laws of economics as expressed by Mises. Trade deficits fail to harm the dollar. The stock market outperforms the economy. Capital gets used up by government and consumers at the expense of investment. Yet business rolls along. Savings are depleted but interest rates stay low. The boom seems unending, the bust postponed indefinitely. Can these phenomena persist?

Absolutely not, says Mises. "Credit expansion is not a nostrum to make people happy. The boom it engenders must inevitably lead to a debacle and unhappiness." He warns, "Accidental, institutional, and psychological circumstances generally turn the outbreak of the crisis into a panic. The description of these awful events can be left to the historians. It is not...(our task)...to depict in detail the calamities of panicky days and weeks and to dwell upon their sometimes grotesque aspects.... The final outcome of the credit expansion is general impoverishment. Some people may have increased their wealth; they did not let their reasoning be obfuscated by the mass hysteria, and took advantage in time of the opportunities offered by the mobility of the individual investor...but the immense majority must foot the bill for the malinvestments and the overconsumption of the boom episode."

Austrian economics rests on the foundation of readily observable human actions. Beings have goals, they set out to attain them; they have individual preferences; and they act within the framework of time. Each person and his or her actions are different and unique. The very nature of human behavior defies economic codification. Mises points out that there are not quantitative constants in human behavior. In his greatest book, Human Action, he developed a rational economic science based on this human factor. At the same time he tweaked the nose of today's highly popular mathematical economics, statistical economics and econometrics. This posturing and economic forecasting he dismissed as little more than poppycock.

In the early 1930s, the Austrian School of economics was on the verge of carrying the day. But in England the publication of John Maynard Keynes' *General Theory of Employment, Interest and Money* provided the rationalizations necessary for politicians and government to spend and inflate endlessly. Until that moment virtually the entire body and history of economic thought stood against such theories. But Keynes' viewpoints fit hand in glove with the mentality of intervention and statism – politicians, economists and governments jumping in bed together to expand their power and influence. Not that Mises was rebutted or that anyone overturned his conclusions – he was simply ignored. How many Americans have ever heard of Ludwig von Mises? How many businessmen know that he placed the girders and underpinnings under free enterprise that cement that system to reason? How many know that he won the moral high ground for capitalism?

Ludwig von Mises, emigrated to the U.S. in 1940. He continued to write and lectured and taught as a visiting professor at NYU. But it was a far cry from his prestige on the continent. Ignored by the media, by the academic community, by business and by government he remained undaunted, a lone figure firm of principle and intellectual courage, a genuine liberal in the classical sense. Professor von Mises is the painstaking architect of the economy of a free society. However, mainstream economists totally ignore his blueprint. He stands far above the current arguments about how the money supply and the economy should be manipulated. For he maintains our greatest error is for government to exert any influence or control over the supply of money, interest rates and the economic system.

We ignore Mises' teachings at our own peril, and he tells us so. "It rests with men whether they will make the proper use of the rich treasure with which this knowledge provides them or whether they will leave it unused. But if they fail to take the best advantage of it and disregard its teachings and warnings, they will not only annul economics; they will stamp out society and the human race."

CHAPTER VII

THE ECONOMICS OF ARMAGEDDON

"With the exception only of the period of the gold standard, practically all governments of history have used their exclusive power to issue money to defraud and plunder the people."

~ Friedrich Hayek

Whenever I'm stuck over something to write in my newsletter I dig out my dog-eared volume of *Human Action* by Ludwig von Mises. This great economist warned time and again about the sorry consequences of our left-wing monetary policies. Before he passed from the scene in 1973, he wrote, "Radical inflationism is an essential feature of the economic ideology of our age." Mises was death on inflating. In 1967 he wrote, "Inflationism is a government policy of increasing the quantity of money in order to enable the government to spend more than the funds provided by taxation and borrowing. Such 'deficit spending' is nowadays, as everybody knows the characteristic signature of the U.S. government's policies." He added, "There is no reason to be proud of deficit spending or to call it progress."

Mises' main complaint against this inflating was the damage it did to the people who saved. "One of the main achievements of the capitalistic system is the opportunity it offers to the masses of citizens to save and thereby improve their material well-being...the value of all kinds of deposits, bonds and insurance policies is inseparably linked to the purchasing power of the dollar. A policy of creeping inflation...is a policy against the vital material interests of the common man. It hurts seriously those judicious and conscientious earners of wages and salaries who are intent upon improving their own and their families' lot by thrift.... It is...diabolic...for more and more government spending to be financed by credit expansion. The bill for such government extravagance is always footed by the most industrious and provident people. It is their claims [savings] that are shrinking with the dollar's purchasing power."

During Mises' lifetime he saw the arguments of John Maynard Keynes become influential. In 1951 Mises wrote, "The triumphs of Lord Keynes' last book, *The General Theory*, was instantaneous… it has become the gospel of the self-styled progressives all over the world." Today many universities teach Keynesian economics exclusively.

Mises also scorned politicians, Treasury and Federal Reserve officials who claimed to be intent on thwarting inflation. "Those who pretend to fight inflation are in fact only fighting the inevitable consequences of inflation, rising prices…. They try to keep prices low while firmly committed to a policy of increasing the quantity of money that must necessarily make them soar." He further warned, "Inflationism is not a variety of economic policies. It is an instrument of destruction; if not stopped very soon, it destroys the market entirely." He wrote, "Continued inflation inevitably leads to catastrophe."

He culminated his arguments against inflating with dire warnings on where the monetary policies of today will lead. Bear in mind that Mises through his many books is recognized as a towering genius in his field. He warned, "It must be remembered that inflation is not a policy that can last. If inflation and credit expansion are not stopped in time, they result in a more and more accelerated drop in the monetary unit's purchasing power, and in skyrocketing commodity prices until the inflated money becomes entirely worthless and the whole government-manipulated currency system collapses. In our age, this has happened to the monetary regime of various countries."

Finally, here are Mises' comments that apply to the Krugmanites, progressive politicians and the Washington monetary gang: "Inflationism cannot last; if not radically stopped in time, it must lead inexorably to a complete breakdown. It is an expedient of people who do not care a whit for the future of their nation and its civilization. It is the policy of Madame de Pompadour, the mistress of the French King Louis XV – *Apres nous le deluge* (after us the deluge)."

Mises explained what happens in a runaway inflation. "The course of progressing inflation is this: at the beginning the inflow of additional money makes the price of some commodities and services rise; other prices rise later. The price rise affects the various commodities and services at different dates and to a different extent…. This first stage of the inflationary process may last for years. While it lasts, the prices of many goods and services are not yet adjusted to the altered money relation. There are still people in the country who will not yet become aware of the fact that they are confronted with a price revolution which will finally result in a considerable rise of all prices, although the extent of this rise will not be the same in the various commodities and services.

"Finally, the masses wake up. They become suddenly aware of the fact that inflation is a deliberate policy and will go on endlessly. A breakdown occurs. The crack-up boom appears. Everybody is anxious to swap his money against 'real' goods, no matter how much money he has to pay for them. Within a very short time, within a few weeks or even days, the things which were used as money are no longer used as media of exchange. They become scrap paper. Nobody wants to give away anything against them.

"It was this that happened with the continental currency in America in 1781, with the French *mandats territoriaux* in 1796, and with the German mark in 1923. It will happen again whenever the same conditions appear. If a thing has to be used as a medium of exchange, public opinion must not believe that the quantity of this thing will increase beyond all bounds."

In March of 1945, Ludwig von Mises gave a speech to a group of intellectuals in Philadelphia. The speech could have been given today. He described the liberal agenda. "The interventionists believe that government has the power to improve the masses' standard of living partly at the expense of the capitalists and entrepreneurs, partly at no expense at all. They recommend the restriction of profits and the equalization of incomes and fortunes by confiscatory taxation, the lowering of the rate of interest by an easy money policy and credit expansion, and the raising of the workers' standard of living by the enforcement of minimum wage rates. They advocate lavish government spending."

Countering this progressive viewpoint, Mises wrote, "Those who pretend that they want to preserve freedom, while they are eager to fix prices, wage rates, and interest rates at a level different from that of the market, delude themselves. There is no other alternative to totalitarian slavery than liberty. There is no other planning for freedom and general welfare than to let the market system work. There is no other means to attain full employment, rising real wage rates and a high standard of living for the common man than private initiative and free enterprise."

Ludwig von Mises was 40 years old when he lived through the great inflation of the Weimar Republic in 1921. This economic tragedy wiped out the savings of the German people. This inflation gave impetus to the Nazis, a fringe movement of extremists at the time. Mises observed Hitler's rise to power and his virulent anti-Semitism. Consequently, Mises who was Jewish closed up shop in Austria and moved to Switzerland just before the Nazis annexed Austria. His books and papers were eventually recovered in Russia many years later. Eventually, he escaped into the south of France, evaded the Nazis and got on a ship to the U.S. He then became a professor at NYU and elsewhere.

In 1949 Mises wrote of his experience in the Weimar era hyperinflation. "The recurrence of periods of economic depression is the outcome of the repeated attempts to improve the operation of capitalism by 'cheap money' and credit expansion. If one wants to avert depressions, one must abstain from any tampering with the rate of interest. Thus was elaborated my theory which supporters and critics soon began to call the 'Austrian theory of the trade cycle.'

"As expected, my theses were furiously vilified by the apologists of the official doctrine. Especially abusive was the response on the part of the German professors. In exemplifying one point, a hypothetical assumption was made [by Mises] that the purchasing power of the German mark might drop to one-millionth of its previous equivalent. 'What a muddle-headed man who dares to introduce – if only hypothetically – such a fantastic assumption!' shouted one of the reviewers. But a few years later the purchasing power of the mark was down not to one-millionth, but to one-billionth of its prewar amount!

"It is a sad fact that people are reluctant to learn from either theory or experience. Neither the disasters brought about by deficit spending and low interest rate policies, nor the confirmation of the theories by such eminent thinkers as Friedrich von Hayek, Henry Hazlitt and the late Benjamin M. Anderson have up to now been able to put an end to the popularity of the fiat money frenzy. The monetary policies of all nations are headed for a new catastrophe.

"Money is the phenomenon of the market, a medium of exchange. But governments think of money as a product of government activity. Money is not a creation of the government. This should be repeated again and again. It is government interference that has destroyed money in the past and it is government interference that is destroying money again…. A thing cannot serve as money if the government has the right to increase its quantity at its pleasure."

Mises not only advocated free markets, he established the moral foundation that underpins capitalism: "The market economy directs the individual's activities into those channels in which he best serves the wants of his fellow man." He also mistrusted the state. "If government were in a position to expand its power *ad libitum*, it could abolish the market economy and substitute for it all-round totalitarian socialism. In order to prevent this, it is necessary to curb the power of government. This is the task of all constitutions, bills of rights, and laws. This is the meaning of all struggles which men have fought for liberty."

Mises was the greatest champion of capitalism the world has ever known. We've condensed some of his writings on why capitalism works so well, as follows:

The characteristic feature of modern capitalism is mass production of goods for consumption by the masses. The result is a tendency towards a continuous improvement in the average standard of living. In a capitalistic society it is the common man or woman whose buying ultimately determines what should be produced in what quantity and quality. Those shops and plants which cater exclusively to the wealthier citizens' demand for refined luxuries play merely a subordinate role in the market economy. They never attain the size of big business. Big business always serves – directly or indirectly – the masses.

The profit system makes those men and women prosper who have succeeded in filling the wants of the people in the best possible and cheapest way. The entrepreneurs and capitalists owe their wealth to the people who patronize their businesses. They lose it as soon as other men or women supplant them in serving the consumers better or cheaper. Wealth can be acquired only by serving the consumers. The consumers determine who should own and run the plants, shops and farms.

Under capitalism everybody's station of life depends on his or her own doing. Capitalism is essentially a system of mass production for the satisfaction of the needs of the masses. It pours a horn of plenty upon the common man. Under capitalism the common man enjoys amenities which in ages gone by were unknown and therefore inaccessible even to the richest people. It has raised the average standard of living to a height never dreamed of in earlier ages. It has made accessible to millions of people enjoyments which a few generations ago were only within the reach of a small elite.

The entrepreneurs who provide the best products and services succeed in getting rich. What counts in the market economy is not academic judgments of value, but the valuations actually manifested by people in buying or not buying. To the grumbler who complains about the unfairness of the market system only one piece of advice can be given: if you want to acquire wealth, then try to satisfy the public by offering them something that is cheaper or which they like better.

CHAPTER VIII

THE WELFARE PROBLEM

"The first requisite of a sound monetary system is that it put the least possible power over the quantity or quality of money in the hands of the politicians.
~ Henry Hazlitt

U p until the 1950's welfare and government doles were frowned on by the public, and to a great extent, by welfare workers and recipients. According to author Marvin Olasky, "Before the push for a Great Society began, recipients themselves often viewed welfare as a necessary wrong.... A sense of shame was relied upon to make people reluctant to accept 'the dole' unless absolutely necessary...as late as the mid-1960's, only about half of those eligible for welfare payments were receiving them..." But liberals were able to secure the levers of political power, and by the end of the 1960's, attitudes changed. Young men were taught that the dole was preferable to a low-paying job. There was no penalty for refusing work. According to a prominent social worker, "Social justice required an end to scrutiny of behavior."

Author Charles Murray tells us, "Throughout the 1970's, the conventional wisdom on the left was that scarcity of jobs was the root problem, and the provision of jobs was the root solution. But several American cities have enjoyed red-hot economies with low skill, good-paying jobs easily available...this economic growth is having almost no effect on the size of the underclass."

Currently, low income households receive $2 trillion annually in redistribution programs. The number of welfare recipients has doubled and redoubled again. Radical organizations established the view that welfare was a right. It was widely thought that with enough money, poverty could be cured. One liberal administration official argued, "The way to eliminate poverty is to give the poor people enough money so that they won't be poor anymore." However the more money that was spent, the worse the problem became.

Author John Perazzo explains, "Since 1965, more than $22 trillion of taxpayer money (in constant 2012 dollars) has been spent on means-tested welfare programs for the poor. The most devastating by-product of the mushrooming welfare state was the corrosive effect it had on American family life. As provisions in welfare laws offered ever-increasing economic incentives for shunning marriage and avoiding the formation of two-parent families, illegitimacy rates rose dramatically. A mother generally received far more money from welfare if she was single rather than married. Once she took a husband, her benefits were instantly reduced by roughly 10 to 20 percent. As a Cato Institute study noted, welfare programs for the poor incentivize the very behaviors that are most likely to perpetuate poverty. The results of welfare policies discouraging marriage and family were dramatic, as out-of-wedlock birthrates skyrocketed among all demographic groups in the U.S. The out-of-wedlock birth rates today stand at 29% for whites, 41% for the nation overall, and 73% for blacks. In other words, the entire country is moving rapidly in the wrong direction, but blacks in particular have reached a point of veritable catastrophe.

"The devastating societal consequences of family breakdown cannot be overstated. Father-absent families generally occupy the bottom rung of America's economic ladder. Regardless of race or ethnicity, the poverty rate for single parents with children is several times higher than the corresponding rate for married couples with children. According to Robert Rector, senior research fellow with the Heritage Foundation, 'The absence of marriage increases the frequency of child poverty 700 percent' and thus constitutes the single most reliable predictor of a self-perpetuating underclass."

Libertarian David Boaz puts it this way, "The stark truth is that as long as the welfare state makes it possible for young women – or teenage girls – to have children without a husband and survive without a job, out-of-wedlock births will remain ruinously high, and the inner city will continue to be marked by crime, poverty, and despair."

Those trapped permanently in the welfare cycle suffer serious character damage. Excused from any requirement to accomplish anything, they experience a stifling boredom, the relief from which too often erupts in self-destructive behavior. Alcoholism and drug addiction are the most prevalent and seemingly inevitable consequence of several generations on welfare.

Peter Drucker sums it up, "Despite ever larger and constantly growing expenditures, the 'welfare mess' in the United States is getting steadily worse. In fact, a strong case can be made – and has been made – that the poor in America...have become the poorer, the more helpless, the more disadvantaged, the more welfare money is being spent to help them. American welfare spending encourages dependence. It paralyzes rather than energizes."

Author Llewellyn H. Rockwell Jr. digs even deeper: "America's 20th century experiment with the welfare state desolated our cities, created a permanent underclass of promiscuity, illegitimacy, welfare and crime, and gave us children and adults full of race hatred instead of the social discipline and work ethic necessary to civilization."

Infants raised by mothers who are addicts, prostitutes, alcoholics, or abusers, grow up without the powerful civilizing force of maternal love. As Murray describes, "(C)hildren unnurtured, undisciplined, sometimes unfed and unwashed...on one occasion ignored, on another laughed at indulgently, and on yet another cursed and beaten." Too often these children grow up to be gang members and criminal predators. Their crimes and the suffering they cause should be laid on the doorsteps of liberals whose runaway urge for social engineering failed to factor in the basic elements of human nature. Author Napoleon Hill said, "Nature does not long tolerate something for nothing." We pay a terrible price for the mistakes of social planners who refuse to examine the consequences of their failing programs.

Common sense tells us that something has gone radically wrong with welfare. Permanent income subsidies are chronically destructive. The problem is out of control. We need to understand what causes the harmful behavior of the subsidized. In 1966, Robert Ardrey wrote a controversial inquiry into the nature of man entitled, *The Territorial Imperative*. He linked behavior with the ownership and defense of territory. (Birds sing to defend their territory.) This contention, and its allusion to private property, made Ardrey unpopular with the left. His wisdom never gained mainstream attention.

He claimed that there are three principal needs of all higher animals, including man: the need for identity, the need for stimulation, and the need for security. Beyond these three, he could find no others. Ardrey wrote, "Identity, stimulation, security; if you will think of them in terms of their opposites their images will be sharpened. Identity is the opposite of anonymity. Stimulation is the opposite of boredom. Security is the opposite of anxiety. We shun anonymity, dread boredom, seek to dispel anxiety. We grasp at identification, yearn for stimulation, conserve or gain security."

"There are few exceptions," he wrote, "to the rule that the need for identity is the most powerful and most pervasive among all species. The need for stimulation is not far behind. And security, normally, will be sacrificed for either of the other two." Then, ominously for the American welfare state he wrote, "The structure of security is the birthplace of boredom.... Our means of satisfying innate needs are precious few, and sacrifice of any must mean replacement by another."

Mankind's requirement to feed, clothe, and shelter themselves fulfills these human needs. Work relieves boredom, and even a humdrum job brings far more stimulation than idleness. Success at a job brings status and identity that relieves anonymity. And security is by definition the result of work and labor.

Social welfare provides security, but deprives the recipient of the stimulation and identity that come from work and struggle. Writing in a biology book in the mid-sixties, almost as though he could foretell the failed future of the "Great Society," Robert Ardrey stated, "We may agree, for example, that our societies must provide greater security for the individual; yet if all we succeed in producing is a social structure providing increased anonymity and ever increasing boredom, then we should not wonder if ingenious man turns to such amusements as drugs, housebreaking, vandalism, mayhem, riots, or – at the most harmless – strange haircuts, costumes, standards of cleanliness, and sexual experiments." Nowhere else has anyone written a more apt description of the welfare predicament.

Work is part of the growth process of life. A job forces people to maintain certain standards of good character, effort, and temperance. If you steal, lie, or take drugs while at work, you lose your job. Welfare does not weaken you as much as it excuses you from the normal pressures of employment and self-sufficiency that make you stronger and improve your character. Economist Thomas Sowell writes, "Achievement is not what liberalism is about. Victimhood and dependency are."

Liberal social programs destroy human initiative. They eliminate the need to struggle and to overcome life's difficulties. Instead of getting tougher and smarter, the subsidized get weaker. Entrepreneurs learn quickly the necessity of struggle and persistence. I encountered what seemed like insurmountable problems in starting a business. However, it turned out that the solution was always available. In my book *The Start-up Entrepreneur*, I quoted Lee De Forest, the inventor of the vacuum tube: "There were some times when I felt as if I had gone my limit. Some of my setbacks were stunners. It seemed as if I couldn't get the stamina to start again. But every time, when I studied things over a little, I would find a way out. No matter how hopeless things look, there is always a way out if you look for it hard enough."

Government programs pull the rug out from under the people they supposedly help. Liberal social programs make people helpless. As motivational author Napoleon Hill put it, "We are forced to recognize that this universal necessity for struggle must have a definite and useful purpose. That purpose is to force the individual to sharpen his wits, arouse his enthusiasm, build up his spirit of faith, gain definiteness of purpose, develop his power of will, inspire his faculty of imagination to give him new uses for old ideas and concepts, and thereby fulfill some unknown mission for which he or she may have been born.

"Strength, both physical and spiritual, is the product of struggle! 'Do the thing,' said Emerson, 'and you shall have the power.' Meet struggle and master it, says nature, and you shall have strength and wisdom sufficient for all your needs. In every form of life, atrophy and death come from idleness! The only thing nature will not tolerate is idleness. There may be some pain in most forms of struggle, but nature compensates the individual for the pain in the form of power and strength and wisdom which come from practical experience."

Hill wrote, "When any individual reconciles himself to the state of mind wherein he is willing to accept largess from the government, instead of supplying his needs through personal initiative, that individual is on the road to decay and spiritual blindness. When a majority of the people of any nation give up their inherited prerogative right to make their own way through struggle, history shows clearly that the entire nation is in a tailspin of decay that inevitably must end in extinction. The individual who not only is willing to live on the public treasury, but demands that he be fed from it, is already dead spiritually."

Liberals are blind to the wisdom in these paragraphs. What's the matter with them? Do they have a death wish for our country? This is the main reason America is in so much trouble. Too many people are taking the easy way out. Progressives have absolutely no insight into the damage they do. Their runaway social sympathy sentences people to a miserable life. The liberal agenda is the blueprint for national ruin.

A century ago an author by the name of Grenville Kleiser wrote these words: "The worst thing that can befall you is to have nothing useful to do. From that moment life will be an aimless, aching void, and time a cruel torturer. The man who has not experienced the joy of hard work has lived in vain. A life of ease and sloth is a daily purgatory and a cause of widespread unhappiness. It is incomprehensible that in this day of golden opportunity there should be anyone, in good health, with nothing to work and live for. The joy of work, of daily conquest, of unexpected difficulties overcome, of new enterprises – these make life interesting, worthwhile and wholesome. Find your right vocation, put your best abilities to daily use, work cheerfully, willingly, and courageously, and you will know the joy of true living."

This poem by Ella Wheeler Wilcox sums it up beautifully:

Three Things

Know this, ye restless denizens of earth,
Know this, ye seekers after joy and mirth,
Three things there are, eternal in their worth.

Love that outreaches to the humblest things;
Work that is glad, in what it does and brings;
And faith that soars upon unwearied wings.

Divine the powers that on this trio wait.
Supreme their conquest, over Time and Fate.
Love, Work, Faith – these three alone are great.

Every once in a while I switch the TV channel from Fox to CNBC to see what the liberals are saying. After listening awhile I get a deep sense of hopelessness and foreboding for our country. The most important thing for the left is giving money to people. They are happy to see the growth of food stamps, disability payments, housing subsidies, free health care and all the other welfare benefits. They utterly fail to see the damage it is doing to the recipients. Neighborhoods that once flourished have deteriorated into festering eyesores populated with homeless people or chemically dependent ne'er-do-wells. These people are no longer employable. They have become incompetent and helpless and the liberals can't see that it's their doing.

Furthermore, each new wave of subsidized citizens (and new immigrants) promises to have some of its members fall into the same behavioral sinkhole – if not them, their offspring who will learn to embrace the subsidized life. We hear only that a bad economy is propelling the growth in government handouts. We never hear that the subsidized life is easier, softer and seemingly without challenge. We never hear that it is the opposite of ambition, struggle and growth.

Bad behavior and low character are common among the welfare underclass. The media plies us with stories aimed to arouse our sympathy for the poor. They overlook that in America today, "poor" stands as much for poor character as it does for poverty. Many of our poor deserve far less sympathy and least of all do they deserve a check. Theirs is not the same kind of poverty that we see in poor African countries where jobs don't exist. Anybody can get a job here as millions of dirt poor immigrants of every racial background prove conclusively. There is a job within walking distance in every American city. While jobs go begging, some people still refuse to work. Why work when you don't have to? It's easier to get a government check.

Author George Gilder sums it up, "The moral hazards of current [social] programs are clear. Unemployment compensation promotes unemployment. Aid for families with dependent children…makes more families dependent and fatherless. Disability insurance in all its multiple forms encourages the promotion of small ills into temporary disabilities and partial disabilities into total and permanent ones. Social Security payments may discourage concern for the aged and dissolve the links between generations…. All means-tested programs…promote the value of being 'poor' (the credentials of poverty), and thus perpetuate poverty."

What do subsidies and welfare have to do with gold, the subject of this book? They are a large component of budgetary and spending excesses. They could not exist without onerous levels of taxation and the continuous inflating of money and credit. Destruction of the money through inflation goes hand in hand with more socialism and less freedom. Debase the money and you also debase the culture. Said another way, welfare payments require a monetary system that finances big government and its interventionist philosophy. Economic retrogression and failure follow that policy. Adoption of this bankrupt philosophy in the U.S. with its potential for civic disruption and runaway inflation represents a forceful argument for gold ownership.

CHAPTER IX
WHITE HEAT

*"Were we to be directed from Washington when to sow and
when to reap, we should soon want bread."*

~ Thomas Jefferson

We're hearing more and more hate-filled comments about white people from the left. Author Andrew Sullivan writes, "Loathing and contempt for white people is now background noise on the left." Another writer on the left tells us that hatred of whites on the "social justice left" is typical. A controversial character at the New York Times, Sarah Jeong, writes "the thing stopping people of color is...a disinclination towards genocide?" Sadly for this dumb cluck instilling hatred in people is how genocide begins.

"The white race," wrote Susan Sontag, "is the cancer of human history." These kinds of racist comments are infuriating. Such sentiments are not only divisive, they can serve as rationalizations for anti-white violence. Underclass criminals would have no problem latching on to this view as justification for property crimes and worse. Frankly, it's disturbing. We need to love and respect the good citizens of all races. Tolerance, generosity and kindness are what makes America great.

The wacky leftist Sarah Jeong writes further, "The world could get by just fine with zero white people." Sorry Sarah, I don't think so. If you want to start comparing accomplishments, here's a few names that have made America prosperous and dramatically improved our living standards. Heaven forbid, they are all white males and capitalists to boot. Ford, Firestone, Dodge, Hershey, Edison, Bell, Whitney, Rockefeller, Heinz, Lipton, Watson, Zuckerman, Walgreen, Carnegie, Drucker, Sloan, Kroc, Marcus, Forbes, Penney, Ogilvy, Bakeland, Disney, Burbank, Wanamaker, Schiff, Sears, Schwab, Field, Geneen, Stone, Giannini, Hilton, Kaiser, Ochs, McCormick, Land, Johnson, Kresge, DuPont, Eastman, Gates, Curtis, Carrier, Kroger, Marriott,

Ketterling, Mellon, Carlson, Statler, Wood, Hewlett, Packard, Luce, Vanderbilt, Salk, Willys, Woolworth, Bezos, Walton, Brin, Busch, Kraft, DeVos, Dell, Remington, Chrysler, Hughes and Honeywell to name a few.

I don't think the world would have got along fine without them and a lot of other old, white (business) men. In fact, you might be living in harsh conditions had they never existed. It's time for responsible progressives to come down hard on this kind of nonsense from the left. Almost every day we are confronted that the left is dividing us. Successful people are now condemned for their prosperity.

Few things are more reprehensible than liberal spokespersons accusing white people of bigotry and racism. The reality is quite the opposite. Outside of a tiny handful of Klan members, the vast majority of white folks are kind, generous and helpful towards minorities. They want minorities to get ahead and try to accommodate them whenever they can. White people are not threatened in the least by the success of minorities and they are glad and proud of minority success. In reality our society bends over backwards to facilitate minorities.

Even more reprehensible is to blame whites (white privilege, institutional racism) for the predicaments of unsuccessful individuals who are minorities. The people locked in poverty, addiction or crime are not there because of whites. Actually minorities were making great strides until midway in the twentieth century. Back then the family unit among minorities was strong, incomes were growing and single parent families were rare. However, all that began to change with the advent of the welfare system.

Minorities who come here from foreign lands have a much higher success rate and reach higher levels of achievement than domestic minorities who are dependent on the welfare system. Whites in no way impede the success of minority immigrants. Successful immigrants sing the praises of the freedom and opportunity America offers. Unfortunately minorities that depend on government subsidies have fallen into a behavioral sinkhole. They are failing and rather than accept any responsibility they are blaming whites and most especially successful whites. The number of young activists who are bamboozled by this sleight of hand should give us all cause for concern.

The people who comprise the upper middle class are the most tolerant, generous and helpful people in the nation. They are the bedrock of American greatness. Their neighborhoods are clean and free of litter. Their lawns are mowed and flowers beautify their yards. The Stars and Stripes are flown on appropriate holidays. Their schools are free of serious disruption and crime rarely visits their neighborhoods. Children can play safely in their own yards. These good citizens go to bed early and rise rested ready for the day's challenges. They work hard and count their blessings. They are honest and trustworthy and possess good character. Without them, our country would be in a shambles. Nevertheless, these good people are accused of intolerance, hatred and greed. They are blamed for the shortcomings of others and the failures in our society. Their attitudes supposedly hold others back. The left call this institutional racism. This is sheer nonsense, but it holds sway in the media and among those who need excuses to hate. These negative depictions are the agenda of liberalism and the left. It is just another of their many falsehoods.

The fact that so many people are being brainwashed to despise rich and successful people is another cause for worry. Wealthy people create jobs. They hire assistants, helpers and workers. Many service jobs will no longer exist if wealth is extinguished. There are few millionaires in impoverished countries. Business success under capitalism enables individual entrepreneurs to become rich while lifting the masses out of poverty. Nothing else has ever worked. Nevertheless, our marvelous system of free enterprise is under constant attack from a ragtag band of misfits, provocateurs, pinko professors and misguided minorities. Among these repugnant radicals are the moneyed liberals of Silicon Valley and elsewhere who fail to see that they will ride the tumbrils to the guillotine before any others. To not understand the greatness of the system that enabled their good fortune and to not see how liberalism will destroy it is both treason and folly.

In recent elections, hedge funds gave millions to left-wing candidates. These are business people. Their knowledge of how capitalism works must be as shallow as water on a mirror. Silicon Valley is thick with liberal nouveau riche. The heads of companies like Starbucks and Costco are lefties. Maybe they have some bleeding heart social scheme that's near and dear to them, but the threat to capitalism is far more important than who gets to use the ladies' bathroom.

Lenin claimed that the capitalists would sell the Bolsheviks the rope they would use to hang them. It's no different when a business person supports political candidates who want to raise taxes and increase government intervention into the private sector. They are dupes endorsing the system that will undermine them. There is no more disgraceful act then to be a traitor to the system that rewarded you and made you prosperous. Left-wing business leaders are the Benedict Arnolds of our time.

Professor Murray Rothbard adds another twist, "While big-business leaders and firms can be highly productive, servants of consumers in a free market economy, they are also all too often, seekers after subsidies, contracts, privileges, or cartels furnished by big government. Often, business lobbyists and leaders are the sparkplugs for the statist, interventionist system."

The America I grew up in was safe, polite, well behaved, moral and friendly. It wasn't just my neighborhood, it was almost every neighborhood. We didn't have people killing themselves with drug overdoses and crime was subdued and rare. The shootings, riots, civil disorders and violent demonstrations of today didn't exist back then. Homelessness was unheard of. What has changed the way people behave in just 60 years?

The government wasn't giving people money back then. Welfare had hardly begun and payments for unemployment, social security disability and a myriad of other government assistance programs didn't exist. You worked hard and that was the only option. Wages were modest and jobs were plentiful. But even on a low wage you could afford to live a comfortable life and raise a family. I know, I did it.

People who suffered hardships turned to private charity or churches for aid. It was a system that left the people unspoiled, law abiding and diligent. Then came the liberal onslaught of free money for life's difficulties. People were able to avoid the consequences of not providing for themselves. Behavior coarsened. From one generation to the next, alcoholism and addiction flourished. Bad parenting, misbehavior and low character began to plague the welfare class. The more money they got, the worse they became.

If you could trace the history of today's shooters and looters, I believe that somewhere in their past or present you'll find the government dole corrupting either their behavior or their parents' behavior. It's a long way from what the mainstream media would have us believe, but it's their liberal policies that have created this mess. Their answer is always to pass out more money. Never mind that it's not working.

You can rightly fear for the future. The subsidized class and their sympathizers could someday vote a Venezuelan-style redistributionist into office. If the welfare payments ever stop, there could be a war on the wealthy. Crimes will be sanctioned. This time the barbarians will be inside the gates.

CHAPTER X
ANECDOTAL EVIDENCE

"We are in a world of irredeemable paper money – a state of affairs unprecedented in history."
~ John Exter

They dropped the boy off at my house one spring day. His mother had poisoned herself with too much whiskey. She was dead at age 41. The boy had stayed with his mom's bleary-eyed boyfriend until the funeral was over. Now his sisters had asked if my wife and I would take him for a few days. They knew that I had sometimes taken the boy fishing. He had no dad. His father had molested the boy's two half-sisters and then skipped town. He had never once called the boy.

The mother had always been on welfare and she'd always been a heavy drinker. She left the boy alone most nights while she sat in a bar. At age four and five he would turn all the lights on, afraid to be alone at night. If a woman loves alcohol or drugs more than her children, her kids suffer for it. Often their emotions will be stunted, their character weakened and their habits irrational. They emulate the dysfunction they see and they learn to be parents unto themselves. By age five or six what ails and disturbs them may no longer be fixed.

The boy was eleven when he came to us. His sisters had lives of their own and the few days he was to stay turned into a few years. He had school problems and we soon got to know a series of grade school and junior-high teachers. Sometimes he seemed devoid of emotion and couldn't seem to resist any wrongdoing that might impress a classmate. A year went by and the welfare department found out the boy was living with us. They couldn't believe we had the boy without them knowing about it. They insisted we go through a process to see if we could qualify as foster parents. They inspected our home. I laughed. The boy had come from a hovel into an expensive home but the social worker criticized the lack of a handrail on one stairway. After wrangling awhile they gave us the boy. By that time his constant misbehaving made us unsure that we wanted him.

Another year passed and one day he stole my Suburban and went for a drive. That was the last straw. We investigated special schools and programs for delinquent boys. We found an Outward Bound program in Montana. We took him to see the place. We liked the school and decided he could spend the year there with thirty other disturbed kids and their counselors. It cost us $30,000 for the year. After eight months the welfare department found out about it. They said we had no right to send him out of state. We weren't taking their money so we disagreed. They got a court order and brought him back. They stuck him in a foster home and took us to court. The judge ruled in our favor. Back went the boy to Montana. The school urged us to keep him there one more year. We agreed, but after a few months they called and said he couldn't stay any longer. He'd worn them out.

They recommended a 30-day program at a hospital in California. It cost $30,000 for the month. We had insurance and in desperation we sent him. After four weeks he came home dressed in leather, several tattoos, earrings and a minor social infection. I wrote the hospital and told them they were running a racket.

He went to live with his sister. They clashed. He moved in with a girl. At age 16 he became a father. He lived off the girlfriend's welfare checks. They split up. Then he got another girl pregnant with her second child. This girlfriend bought him a car with her welfare check. It soon quit running. He needed money to buy a mobile home for his new family. I gave him the down payment. Within a few months they lost the place. He got a job but quit after the first paycheck. Another guy moved in with them. After a few months he found the two of them together and moved out.

He called me soon after. The first girlfriend had dropped off their daughter while she went to get something to eat. She'd been gone for three days. Now he was growing tired of baby-sitting and being a dad. I called around and got him a couple of job interviews. He didn't make them. He's nineteen with a clouded future. You'll probably never read about the boy in the newspapers. He's not a hardened criminal like so many products of welfare. But unless something changes his life will always be a mess. Unfortunately, the government encourages him and the young girls he cohabitates with to have kids. The more children, the more money. Supposedly we do this for the children. But they benefit the least.

The press likes to depict the poor as being just like the people next door but with a run of bad luck. If those writers could actually live next door to the poor they would soon quit their sympathetic stories. Twenty-five years ago I bought an apartment building in a transitional neighborhood. The realty agent lied about the tenants. The renters were of all races and they shared a common trait. They rarely paid their rents. On the outside it was a nice looking building but on the inside it was a disaster. The security company I hired to install a buzzer system on the front door quit in disgust. Every time the installer went out to his truck for a part someone stole everything he had left inside.

The tenants wrecked the apartments. They stole whatever they could. They disfigured the walls and the floors. They slept on mattresses on the floor and hung sheets over windows. They lied about the rent and they skipped out without paying. One evening I tried to collect some overdue rent. Two women were in one apartment with two cute little girls about three and four. Right in front of my eyes the mother gave each child a couple of puffs of marijuana and sent them off towards bed. I was dumbfounded. A few days later a city inspector called me to come pick up the garbage on the boulevard. Instead I called the Realtor and put the place up for sale.

We should rely on our own experience to draw conclusions about the poor. Government-sponsored solutions are doomed from the start. Expensive counseling, job training, treatment programs and other billion dollar pipe-dreams won't work. If love and nurturing and good examples are replaced by abuse, indifference and bad examples, all the government programs on earth won't help the children. Therein lies the rub. How do we resolve the greatest problem ever created by mankind? How do we overcome resistance from the left? How do we take something away from those who count on it without an explosion of crime and rioting? How do we get the politicians to sense the enormity of this problem? How do we turn this shattered system around?

Don't ask the left. When confronted with the huge behavioral problems of the welfare underclass, liberals have no workable solution. They want more government programs and more money handed out. Unfortunately, the behavioral problems of the subsidized class are growing worse in spite of all the governments financial help.

A new drug treatment facility is being built on a Minnesota reservation where the alcoholism rate runs as high as 90%. Opiate deaths among Native Americans in our state are six times higher than the general population. What chance do kids have for a better life when their parents are drug addicts and alcoholics or both? The truth of the matter is that kids with bad parents would be better off if they were removed to another environment.

A few years ago a woman who was renowned in our state for helping the poor proposed building an orphanage in a suburb of Minneapolis. Liberals went nuts arguing against the idea. The local newspaper wrote numerous editorials condemning her. She was attacked so bitterly, she abandoned the idea.

Liberals hurt poor kids more than they help them. In the Minnesota legislature liberals passed a law making it nearly impossible for white families to adopt Indian kids. In a sense, little kids with bad parents are trapped. Instead of going to college, they go to a treatment center. Removing kids from worthless parents (even to orphanages) is the only solution. Unfortunately, this will never happen because the left won't allow it. Liberals insist on the status quo for the welfare class. Maybe it's just a matter of votes.

No problem-free way to end these subsidies exist. But not ending them begs disaster. The quality of our life hinges on stopping the growth of dependency and shoring up families and sound values. Either we terminate welfare or it will terminate our way of life. Halfway measures will invariably succumb to political pressure, media exposure, social sympathy, bureaucratic incompetence, economic slowdowns, and complaints by the recipients. A laboratory in which to study the long- term effects of welfare subsidies exists in the Native American reservations of the northern prairie states and Canada. My experiences here provide more anecdotal evidence. These people have been getting welfare or treaty money for as long as 175 years. They have been isolated on reservations devoid of opportunities for advancement or payoffs for their efforts.

I turned my mud-covered Suburban onto the gravel road leading through the reservation. In the back two mallards lay on a bag of decoys. They had flown into the Saskatchewan pothole I had hunted earlier that day. I planned to give them to Bird Lady. Each year I dropped off a few plump mallards for Bird Lady and her daughters. It was close to one in the afternoon when I turned up Bird Lady's driveway. Her house sat on the top of a knoll a quarter-mile off the main gravel. I passed the run-down bungalows of her daughters and pulled into the barren, weedy yard. A dozen oversized chickens scurried away. I walked up the porch steps and knocked on the door. No one came. I thought about Bird Lady as I waited. She had been a beautiful woman once, but the ravages and alcohol had withered her beyond her years. I pounded louder. It quickly dawned on me that I had come too early. Bird Lady slept and she would not get up now.

I glanced at the daughters' modern bungalows that had not been kept up. Rags were stuffed into holes in windows and siding. Curtains, towels and sheets covered the windows. A beat-up car sat in front of one. Neither would the daughters rise. In past years I had noted that the daughters showed signs of advanced alcoholism. Their appearance had deteriorated. They could never seem to look me in the eye and although I had tried to engage one of them in conversation her hang-dog expression revealed a sense of inferiority. Their children were in school today. On weekends the children would be outside in the morning at unsupervised play while the elders slept. It was that way across this and many other reservations.

In all of rural America nothing is sadder than the reservations. They are laboratories for a social experiment that has damaged the character and skill of people who were once the most self-sufficient on earth. Never in history has an entire category of people been gripped by such levels of helplessness and addiction. A mailer I received from a Native American charity claimed that the alcoholism rate on Minnesota reservations is 90%.

Responsibility for this predicament does not lie solely with the 7th Cavalry or the gory spectacle at Wounded Knee and elsewhere. It lies with liberal social scientists and politicians who have insisted on giving these people a monthly stipend that left them unchallenged, unmotivated and bored senseless. Subsidies diminish human potential. They are a national disgrace. I rolled the Suburban down the drive, away from Bird Lady and her daughters. I passed dozens of other bungalows, some occupied, some abandoned or destroyed. No cars passed me. No one would be up yet. I turned it over in my mind. They must go to bed close to dawn. What weird behavioral syndrome does welfare unleash that keeps these people and many others on the permanent dole up until 4 or 5 in the morning, and asleep until the afternoon? How can they raise children on such a schedule?

The dirty little secret is that sometimes the children raise themselves. The little children, who crave love and nurturing, get little or no attention. They play outside through the day, a bag of chips for breakfast, a Pepsi and a Ho-Ho for their lunch, unsupervised and too often neglected.

The liberal Minneapolis Star Tribune reported on a recent tragedy on a northern Minnesota reservation. Two young Native American boys ages four and two wandered away from home last November and went missing. They were found this spring frozen solid. They had wandered through 75 yards of woods, crossed a small lake on the ice and fell into open water on the far shore. In reporting on the story, a reporter depicted the four-year-old as "bold and adventurous." The two-year-old "loved tagging along with his older brother." A spokesman for the reservation commented, "Now we know where they are." Nothing was written about what in the world a preschooler and a toddler were doing wandering around on their own in the winter. There was no mention of parental neglect or wrongdoing. Two unsupervised little kids died because of negligence and we can't get a liberal writer to pen a single criticism. In the eyes of liberals, minorities can do no wrong. But they can. The Associated Press carried this recent story: "On just a single day this year on the Red Lake Reservation in northern Minnesota, police and investigators received emergency calls about a suicide, a murder, three stabbings, two shootings and multiple incidents of domestic violence."

A few years ago, they changed the name of Columbus Day in Minneapolis to Indigenous Peoples' Day. That probably made liberals feel good. Unfortunately, it did nothing to solve the horrible social problems affecting indigenous peoples. The left postures about changing the name of a holiday or a football team while Native Americans sink further into behavioral chaos.

A few months ago, a local sportswriter was beating the drum to change the name of the Washington Redskins. He and his ilk had previously been successful in eliminating the "Fighting Sioux" logo from the University of North Dakota. I sent him the following email: "With a 90% rate of alcohol and drug addiction on reservations and shocking levels of child abuse and crime, it makes a lot of sense to focus on names like Fighting Sioux and Redskins. Nice priorities."

He responded, "You don't see a link between the institutional racism that preserves those nicknames and the institutional racism that preserves those living conditions? I think they are all connected. Of course the abuses and crime are far more serious than a nickname, but it's all related."

I countered, "I don't know what institutional racism is. The racism that led to the reservation system is long gone. Do you mean that nowadays we dislike Indians? Please. The behavioral pathologies on the reservation are the same as those on the near north side. That evolved from the government giving people money. Subsidies caused the misbehavior that's so prevalent. It has nothing to do with racism."

He sent his answer, "That entire email seems to come from such an extreme position of white privilege that all I can say is I disagree in every way and am done debating this with you."

Are liberals blind? At South Dakota's Pine Ridge reservation, population 40,000, there are 3,000 child abuse cases each year. In addition there are 20,000 arrests each year, one for every other person. A tribal officer reports, "We pick up a guy for some alcohol-related offense and are out of town for an hour taking them to jail, and in the meantime people are here clubbing and stabbing each other."

Twenty years ago I stood in the parking lot of a restaurant in The Pas, a small community in Northern Manitoba. I was fishing with a friend and I waited outside while he used the washroom. A large bus had pulled into the lot and disgorged its passengers. The front door of the bus was open, the driver reading a newspaper. Suddenly around the corner came a small Indian boy of about four. He was dressed neatly in shorts and he was a child of such remarkable beauty that my eyes became glued to him. He walked to the bus and stood in the sunlight, looking up into the doorway, fascinated by what he saw. Around the corner came his father. I glanced his way but riveted my attention back on the boy. The father encouraged him to take a few steps onto the bus. It was clear the boy had never entered a bus before and this was a high adventure for him. He took a step up and then another and surveyed the interior of the bus. As he stepped back down I stood fascinated by his handsome demeanor and his curiosity that had prompted this interesting episode.

His father called to him and I looked back at the man. It startled me. The father was my age. Like the boy, he too had been handsome, but too much whiskey had left heavy lines and creases in his face. His red and sunken eyes stared out from his damaged features and his curled posture spoke of intoxication. I looked back at the boy and in a moment of dread I saw what this little angel would likely become. I stood silently and fought the tears.

From the beginning Native Americans were at a huge disadvantage. They relied on arrows, slings and snares and their utensils were of clay. The white interlopers had tools and equipment that fascinated the Indians; items they would want desperately. Imagine it; guns, traps, metal bowls and utensils, needles, cloth, axes, beads and whiskey. Some would trade furs, some would trade land. Gifts and bribes to the Indians became a way of life along the frontier. In the end they lost their land, were forced onto reservations and agreed to behave for money and goods. They made treaties which provided them with food and cash doles. The great Sioux uprising of 1863 that took the lives of over 400 Minnesota settlers flared up because of late payments of food and other broken promises.

Once upon a time there was a simple, honest, self-sufficient tribal culture. It exists no more. The white man ruined that. However, it was not the loss of their land or the subtle imprisonment on reservations that did in the Native Americans and their culture. It was the monthly checks. Subsidies act as behavioral poison.

My friend Bird Lady would have been a different person had she been required to make her own way in life. She had the potential. You could see the intelligence and humor in her eyes. She liked my visits. She could have been somebody. What a waste.

Yes, there are exceptions to Bird Lady. A few Indians farm and work successfully. But the mind-numbing rate of alcoholism on the reservations undermines their potential.

Of the many reservations I have passed through in Canada and the U.S., two stand out. One I flew over in Alaska and was struck by the colossal amount of paper, cardboard and junk spread around and beyond the main village. The pilot remarked about the high alcoholism rate here. Another reservation I visited in Saskatchewan seemed different than the others. There were no junk cars and no empty houses left standing. The yards were manicured and there was no sign of refuse. I politely inquired what was going on here. They told me they were Mormons. The entire population of the reservation were Mormons. As you know, Mormons don't drink or use stimulants or drugs. It was impressive.

The gambling casinos have provided employment for a few Native Americans which is all to the good. They were awarded casinos to make up for their harsh treatment. However, I don't agree with the history that places all the blame for the evils that befell the Indians on the United States. The left is quick to blame our country for the extermination of millions of aborigines. That's a falsehood. The U.S. had nothing to do with most of it. When Columbus set sail, the population of Indians was 35 to 40 million. Most of these were Aztecs, Mayans and Incas centered in Mexico, Central and South America. The Spaniards conquered them, brutalized them and enslaved them. They infected them with smallpox and other diseases that decimated their population. You can say the Europeans should have never come, but it was inevitable. Spaniards were also responsible for the extermination of Florida tribes like the Colusa. Florida was Spanish until 1819.

In the U.S. the native population was small, perhaps as low as one million. Many of the Indian Wars had witnesses among the whites on the number of Native Americans present for battle. They were never able to martial large numbers of warriors. Only 1,500 braves were at the Battle of Tippecanoe. Less than a thousand fought at Fallen Timbers where 40 were killed. These were among the major battles from the French and Indian War (1754-1763) through the war of 1812, a period of great brutality on both sides and of great property loss to the Indians. The Sioux chief Red Cloud managed to put together a fighting force of 4,000 Lakota Sioux, Cheyenne and Arapaho. The Seven Tribes of the Iroquois totaled 10,000 members. Around 14,000 Cherokees were forced west in the "Trail of Tears." One-hundred-and-fifty Sioux were killed at Wounded Knee (and 31 soldiers). The Comanche, the dominant tribe on the southern plains numbered 20,000 to 30,000. Casualties in all the Indian wars within the U.S. amounted to 30,000 Indians and 10,000 whites. These low figures refute claims that the U.S. was responsible for millions of deaths.

That's not to say that smallpox, measles and flu did not kill significant numbers of Native Americans in the U.S. So did destroying their food stores, forcing them to flee their villages and disrupting their hunting grounds. Coping with manipulative whites also took its toll. On the other hand, these natives could be brutal beyond measure and brought hatred to bear on themselves through their torture, kidnapping and raids that killed settlers. For example, after

Braddock was defeated at Fort Duquesne (what now is Pittsburgh) in 1755 a number of British prisoners were taken by the Indians.

In his book *Wilderness Empire*, Allan W. Eckert describes the scene. "It was about sundown that the last of them came in – a smaller group prodding before them twenty or thirty prisoners, including at least half a dozen of the women that had followed Braddock's army across the river…. The faces and upper bodies of half of them had been smudged with charcoal, and James Smith knew it was the mark of the *Cut-ta-ho-tha* – the mark of the condemned.

"The prisoners were marched to the river bank and taken across to the Ottawa and Chippewa camps on the west bank of the Allegheny directly opposite the fort. With a fascination bred of horror, Smith watched posts being erected and a dozen of the blackened men were tied to them. Roaring fires were quickly built around them – not close enough to burn them with living flame, but close enough so that little by little their skin cooked and blistered and then charred. It was a process that took hours and the hideous cries of the tortured men reached peaks of frenzied intensity as flaming brands and red-hot ramrods were poked at their eyes and mouth and genitals."

Hard to believe but some of the surviving prisoners experienced still worse outcomes. Events like this explain why hatred boiled over on the Ohio Frontier. We only hear about the evils that the U.S. visited upon our Native Americans. However, the Indians were often mistreated in response to their savagery. That led to the injustices of the reservation system and the behavioral predicament of today. The blame-America crowd has got it mostly wrong.

CHAPTER XI
PARENTS OF THE YEAR

"No other commodity enjoys as much universal acceptability and marketability as gold."
~ Hans F. Sennholz

We condensed a recent news article in the Minneapolis newspaper:

"Multiple children were drinking alcohol and some were reportedly smoking marijuana in the house where a 3-year-old girl was found Monday night with a 0.12 percent blood-alcohol level. The children's mothers are sisters, ages 32 and 31, each have six children ranging from 1 to 15. The petitions in juvenile court describe a chaotic scene where police found the toddler unresponsive, 'fresh vomit all over the house' and drunken adults yelling to each other.

"The 3-year-old drank Windsor Canadian whiskey after the girl's 14-year-old brother gave it to her in a cup and said it was juice, court documents said. A 5-year-old daughter told authorities that she and three cousins, two of whom are 4 and 6, also drank alcohol. According to court documents: Police officers noticed a 'thick haze of smoke' and a strong smell of marijuana in the home. Children were smoking marijuana. Officers also found liquor spilled on the floor and soiled clothes and food strewn about the house. The 3-year-old's eyes were wide open but were glazed over and she was unresponsive.

"Officers found a juvenile male who appeared intoxicated and smelled strongly of alcohol crawling out a window. Adults home at the time – police have said there were four – were drunk and unable to dress the children. One mother was previously convicted of second-degree murder in 1997 and sentenced to five years in prison in the stabbing death of a woman. She has been the subject of five child-protection reports dating to 2000, including a finding of sexual abuse and endangerment regarding one of her daughters. The other mother's record includes theft convictions. She had multiple contacts with County Child Protection, most stemming from domestic assaults."

If you think preschoolers smoking marijuana are a rarity, you're wrong. It's not uncommon among the urban underclass. That says nothing about sexual promiscuity, thievery, drug peddling and violence among pre-teens and young adults. It's a social mess of staggering proportions brought to you by our liberal social thinkers and bureaucrats. Some social agencies are so incompetent, they will not remove an innocent child or even a tiny infant from abusive, chemically dependent mothers with scumbag boyfriends. Sexual and physical abuse goes unreported and ignored. These brutes are killing infants and children accidentally or on purpose with alarming frequency. Unfortunately, little kids who survive these toxic mothers, relatives and boyfriends are likely to grow up to be hoodlums themselves. This is the circle of dependency and crime that government is purchasing for you with your own money. Your tax dollars fund social programs that produce grossly dysfunctional criminals and addicts. Unfortunately, your grandchildren face the prospect of life among swelling numbers of remorseless criminals.

Our cities are full of similar horror stories. Social programs that pay unwed mothers for each child they have only encourages the least responsible to have multiple births. Some of these mothers are unfit to raise children. There's a million little kids in our country whose character is being ruined by lack of love, chaotic behavior and bad example. Alcoholics, drug addicts, prostitutes and criminals are not fit to raise children. Social workers should be tarred and feathered if they leave babies with these lowlifes. If you took these infants away from the clowns raising them and put them in good homes, twenty years from now they'd be graduating from college instead of going to prison.

We're worrying about the wrong things in this country. What could be more important than protecting little children from criminally negligent adults? What could be more important than transferring kids from behavioral hellholes into loving, secure homes or even orphanages. Prohibitions against interracial adoptions are the insane handiwork of liberal social workers. The American people will step up and save some of these children if given a chance. For that to happen, the progressives must see the gravity of the problem and admit their policies have caused this social mayhem. Frankly, I think they would rather turn their back on these kids than admit their socialist claptrap is bankrupt.

Child welfare workers are mostly liberal. They often push to have abused and endangered children reunited with their worthless parents. For example, a Minneapolis mother convicted of prostitution, drug crimes and other offenses who lost rights to two children due to frequent maltreatment was reunited with her two-year-old son by order of the county.

As a newborn the baby tested positive for high levels of opiates and cocaine. Foster parents weaned him off the drug with methadone as he cried in pain. Nevertheless, the infant was sent back to his mother. When presented with evidence of the mother's continued drug use and prostitution, the county refused to intervene. Recently, the mother was advertising her availability as a prostitute and had the boy with her when she was arrested with four others in a hotel room strewn with dirty needles, crack pipes, cocaine and meth. The boy was then passed around to four or five people and the county lost track of him. Eventually the father was arrested for an unrelated crime and directed police to relatives who had the boy. Hopefully, the foster parents who want to adopt him will get the boy back. Believe it or not the court may still return him to his mother.

When you multiply stories like this thousands of times you get a sense of how much behavioral damage liberal social policies cause. Criminals and addicts who should never raise a child are given this responsibility time and again by social workers and the courts. If you wanted to raise a crop of hoodlums and gangsters this is how you do it.

Author John Perazzo explains, "Children in single-parent households are burdened not only with economic, but also profound social and psychological, disadvantages. For example, youngsters raised by single parents, as compared to those who grow up in intact married homes, are more likely to be physically abused; to display emotional disorders; to smoke, drink, and use drugs; to perform poorly in school; to be suspended or expelled from school; to drop out of high school; to behave aggressively and violently; to be arrested for a juvenile crime; to serve jail time before age 30; and to go on to experience poverty as adults. According to the National Fatherhood Initiative, 60% of rapists, 72% of adolescent murderers, and 70% of long-term prison inmates are men who grew up in fatherless homes."

Is there anything worse that can befall a country than a financial catastrophe and depression? Yes, and it's happening right now. At least 100,000 new criminal predators are coming on to our streets this year. These juvenile delinquents under 20 years old are in an age group known to be more violent than any other. For the most part, they originate within the underclass and are comprised of all races. Statistics are cloudy, but the number of them committing crimes could actually be as high as 250,000 and, worst of all, this is a trend that will continue to grow. In addition, six million people who served time in prison are out on the street, and over half of them are going back to jail. Meanwhile, our penitentiaries are stuffed full with one-and-a-half million inmates.

Many of the underclass never get into trouble with the law themselves, but their dysfunctional behavior gets passed on to the next generation who may then resort to crime. We're not talking about some small slice of the population here, we're talking about a large, growing problem that no modern nation has ever had to cope with. Already, 32% of young black males will be incarcerated at least once. By some estimates, as many as 40% of the male population in the inner city will be ensnared in the criminal justice system. Unemployment in our central cities runs to 60% or higher. That's because normal employment opportunities are too often rejected, while illegal activities in the underground economy flourish.

Crime statistics indicate that children of single parents turn to delinquency at a higher rate. That makes it all the more worrisome that the percentage of children born out of wedlock among the underclass has reached levels that are beyond disgraceful. According to author Mona Charen, "In 1960, the white rate of illegitimacy was 2 percent. In 1999, the rate was 27 percent. Among blacks, the 1960 rate was 23 percent. By 1999, it had climbed to near 70 percent. In some black neighborhoods, children can grow up without knowing anyone who is married." Read that last sentence again and ask yourself what kind of behavioral nightmare are these social programs creating? Mona Charen points out the reason: "(L)iberals...provided young women with the wherewithal (their own apartments and a monthly stipend) to make getting along without a husband possible, and to immature eyes, even desirable."

Writing in the Wall Street Journal editorialist Jason Riley makes a salient point. "Racial gaps that were steadily narrowing in the 1940s, '50s and '60s would expand in the 1970s, '80s and '90s, which suggests that the disparities that continue today aren't being driven by racism, notwithstanding claims to the contrary from liberals and their allies in the media. It also suggests that attitudes toward marriage, education, work and the rule of law play a much larger role than the left wants to acknowledge. More marches won't address out-of-wedlock childbearing. More sit-ins won't lower black crime rates or narrow the school achievement gap.

"A generation of blacks who have more opportunity than any previous generation are being taught that America offers them little more than trigger-happy cops, bigoted teachers and biased employers. Black activists and liberal politicians stress racism because it serves their own interests, not because it serves the interests of the black underclass."

Unfortunately, the underclass of all races has a birth rate approximately three times higher than the general populace. Project those growth rates a few decades into the future and you should be terrified as to what kind of dangerous society your grandchildren will inherit. When a half million teenage hoodlums hit the streets every year, the cities will be worse than war zones. But don't expect the liberals, whose social programs created this mess, to see the error of their ways.

The website Zero Hedge carried a story that sounds like a solution progressives invented: "Lonnie Holmes, 21, lives in Richmond, a working-class suburb north of San Francisco. Four of his cousins have died in shootings. He was a passenger in a car involved in a drive-by shooting, police said. And he was arrested for carrying a loaded gun. When Holmes was released from prison last year, officials in this city offered something unusual to try to keep him alive: money. They began paying Holmes as much as $1,000 a month not to commit another gun crime."

Liberals are great for broadcasting improvement in any small aspect of the crime rate. They downplay crime and mislead us on crime statistics. The day will come when murder doesn't make the newspapers. That's because liberals suspect there might be linkage between giving people money they didn't earn and their behavior. Hello! Liberals don't want to take the blame for a behavioral disaster of this magnitude, but they are responsible.

CHAPTER XII
SLIPPERY SLOPE

"Of all the contrivances for cheating the laboring classes of mankind, none has been more effective than that which deludes them with paper money."
~ Daniel Webster

They have intensive care units in hospitals now specifically for newborn babies that are having problems. It's expensive. I know, because my new granddaughter spent three days there. It was over $30,000. There was another baby there born premature. He was a crack baby and weighed only two pounds. The nurse said he'd be there up to five months. Later I thought about the bill for this tiny infant struggling for life. It would cost about $1,200,000 and the state would have to pay it. Then I thought some more about the kind of life he would have. With a drug-addicted mother, there was little chance he would get the love and nurturing necessary to be a well-adjusted and productive person. More likely he would be in trouble with the law and have his own problems with drugs and alcohol.

No doubt his mother would continue to rely on the government to pay for raising him. She would get aid for her dependent children, public housing, health care and food stamps. When you add all the assistance up, it would probably run close to $25,000 a year for him. That would go on for twenty years or so until he began to get assistance directly. Then he would get the same benefits his mother received including subsidized rent and a welfare check. If he wanted to claim that he suffered from depression, he could get another $1,200 a month from Social Security. Should he take the time to file a tax return, he could get another welfare payment at tax time. Chances are he'd be in and out of the court system. That's also costly. He would need a public defender, court time, incarceration, a parole officer, and the continued attention of the police. As an adult he would probably require at least $50,000 a year in social expenditures. Should he live to age 70, that's a total of $4,200,000 in social costs for him. These are rough estimates, but you get the picture.

There are millions of dependent people in similar circumstances in America. Their numbers are growing dramatically. What you subsidize you get more of. In addition, the U.S. government imports poor immigrants, some of whom begin to rely on social programs permanently. Once these expensive programs are in place they are almost impossible to stop. They change the culture. There's no way to go back. Social programs are a slippery slope. Once they take root they grow until they are unaffordable and irreversible. Eventually their runaway costs can ruin a nation.

Author Martin Dunkin writes, "The welfare state has bred a generation of obnoxious, drug-addled criminals and ne'er-do-wells. It has also, incidentally, burdened what was once the world's biggest, most dynamic economy with the dead weight of an obstructive and vastly expensive state machine."

I fret about what would happen to our country if the left gets voted into power. Since they believe that the cure for poverty is to give more money to the poor, government spending would jump dramatically. I read that there currently are 496 federal programs that give money to the poor. To keep all this going and add more would require higher taxes. The left would cause taxes to rise so high it would begin to kill our economy. Less revenue would cause them to raise taxes even higher.

The more people that are on the dole, the more likely the left will stay in power and move farther left. That's the Venezuelan model. Business people who create wealth are ruined while leftist bureaucrats fatten on what they steal. If you don't think these radicals and socialists would alter or ignore the Constitution you are mistaken. History verifies that leftists will act criminally to stay in power. Nor will liberals ever see or admit their policy failures no matter how egregious.

This country has never before experienced the number of homeless we now have in our cities. Part of this is because the liberals emptied our institutions. I suspect that it's also because the homeless have money. It costs plenty to sit in a makeshift tent and shoot up heroin or snort coke and meth every day. This homeless explosion really got rolling when Social Security granted disability payments to so many. That's about $1,200 a month on top of whatever other state or federal welfare payments they get. That's enough to be comfortably homeless.

A few years ago I wrote a letter to Anna Quindlen, a liberal Newsweek columnist. She had mentioned the positive charity work of the nuns. "How nicely you put it," I wrote. "'Touch the sick, the poor, the children, the powerless...' However, what you liberals forget is that you've taken charity out of private hands and turned it over to the government. That has engineered a social disaster. How many hundreds of blocks in your city or mine are you afraid to walk through on a summer evening? Giving people money that they didn't earn is the worst thing you can do to them. You have a blind spot about the sorry consequences of your social sympathy. You liberals refuse to see the horror and the magnitude of it because of your complicity."

The consequences of social welfare need to be recognized as America's greatest problem. Each day thousands of new infants are born who have no chance of being normal or productive. Their parents doom them from the start. Financial and economic problems can somehow be overcome. Social problems of the kind we have in America cannot be overcome. When a small child is ruined, they are generally ruined for life. Nobody's addressing these problems. Government just keeps getting bigger, always spending more to keep the welfare advocates appeased. In time we will be swept into the vortex of a financial crisis brought on by the government's deficits and the inflationary effect of the money created to pay the tab.

In 1946, the U.S. began to send monthly checks to inhabitants of an island in the Pacific that was next to an atomic bomb testing site. These self-sufficient islanders fished as a way of life. "Sixty Minutes" did a segment on these people after forty years of living on the dole. Since they had no need to fish anymore, many had forgotten how to fish. With no requirement to do anything, their alcohol consumption skyrocketed and social problems set in. Piles of beer cans and other junk marred the island's appearance. It's now known as the slum of the Pacific.

Remove the demand to make our own way and behavior deteriorates. It's hardly an original thought. They've been writing about it for centuries. "An idle man's brain is the devil's workshop," wrote Bunyan. "I look at indolence as a sort of suicide," wrote Chesterfield. Beecher said, "If you are idle you are on the road to ruin, and there are few stopping places upon it. It is rather a precipice than a road." Emerson wrote, "He is base – and that is the one base thing in the universe – to receive favors and render none." Timeless proverbs express the absolute wisdom of the ages. "Idleness rusts the mind." "To do nothing teaches to do ill." "Industry is the parent of virtue." "Idleness is the root of all evil." "He becometh poor that dealeth with a slack hand." "It is a great weariness to do nothing."

Two hundred and fifty years ago the religious thinker Emanuel Swedenborg described a process which goes on today in subsidizing the worst elements of society. "It is believed by many that love to the neighbor consists in giving to the poor, in assisting the needy, and in doing good to every one; but charity consists in acting prudently, and to the end that good may result. He who assists a poor or needy villain does evil to his neighbor through him; for through the assistance which he renders he confirms him in evil, and supplies him with the means of doing evil to others."

Every day incalculable numbers of children in our country are abused. They witness violence, mayhem and depravity. They hear vile language and often they go unsupervised, free to use drugs and keep the hours they choose. Twenty-five million children live in homes without fathers. Two million have parents in prison. How is it that a problem of this magnitude, surely the greatest problem facing any nation, could be such a neglected topic?

In order to confront this behavioral disaster, the left would have to admit responsibility for engineering social programs that have gone astray. They meant to do good, but they did harm. It's not easy for them to admit that their epic social blunder has ruined the character of so many people. So there is little or no hope that anything will change. We will continue to take increasing amounts of money from those who earned it and give it to increasing numbers of those who didn't. Unfortunately, the recipients will be the worse for it. Does anybody seriously think this is going to have a good ending?

CHAPTER XIII

A TRILLION HERE, A TRILLION THERE

"Credit excesses have many parallels in history, but those in the United States are of such extreme magnitude that they suggest a form of collective, manic euphoria."

~ Kurt Richebächer

The following quote was taken from the dust jacket of my book, *Full Faith and Credit: A Novel about Financial Collapse*:

"A sudden decline in the dollar leads to a steep correction in the stock market. As negative economic news piles up, financial markets go from bad to worse, sending stocks and bonds into a relentless tailspin. A panic ensues. The stock market collapses further and most investors are wiped out. The booming economic expansion turns into a sharp credit contraction and depression. Consumer buying shrivels and business activity plummets. Mortgage foreclosures are epidemic. Unemployment soars.

"The worst is yet to come. The dollar crashes, interest rates scream upward, mutual funds postpone redemptions and liquidity vanishes. Massive derivative defaults capsize banks and hedge funds. Huge government guarantees and bailouts put immense financial strains on the government. The depression dramatically reduces the government's tax revenues. Trillions in government debt must be rolled over at double-digit interest rates. A default appears imminent.

"The president meets with the chairman of the Federal Reserve and the secretary of the Treasury to try to fashion a way out of the greatest financial crisis in history."

Certainly this is a gloomy forecast, but others agree there could be problems ahead.

A letter written to Congress by Business Roundtable, a prestigious group of business leaders, had this to say: "In the brief period of the past decade, we have amassed trillions of dollars of debt; we have regressed from being the largest creditor nation in the world to the biggest debtor; we have witnessed the federal deficit absorb over half our net private savings; we have become increasingly dependent upon foreign capital, inexorably ceding our influence over both our domestic and international policies. And we have embarked upon a course which cannot be sustained without high costs – economic, social and human."

Financial advisor Michael Aronstein, then with Comstock Partners, warned in a Barron's Weekly interview: "The natural cyclicality of the economy, cycles of exuberance and depression, has been completely overridden by the government's indemnification of the whole financial sector. Which means you can't have small accidents any more. There are all these artificial, risk-avoidance statutes on the books. They have a whole mythology of risk less finance: Don't worry, this is too big to fail. The government will prevent this from happening. Nobody has ever lost money in an insured deposit. Nobody has ever lost money in a money-market fund because the Fed would never permit it. All of this nonsense was based on the assumption that the reckless deployment of credit can be glossed over by government's willingness to step in and utilize its credit rating.

"And at some point there will be an admission of the inability of government to live up to its financial promises. Not in terms of sustaining people's income, but of guaranteeing the value of all these financial assets that it guarantees. We are about to discover that all of these promises made by government pertaining to finance are empty. Government is having to back away from more and more of its promises. Whether it is a promise to keep the streets safe or the promise to try and give every kid a decent, safe education – whatever, they can't meet these promises.

"All these promises about retirement will be broken. You know, if you work for your 35 years you can retire comfortably and the next generation will pay for it through Social Security. And you can have your bank deposits earn high interest with no risk because they'll pay for it if your bank does something silly. And they will insure everybody's medical care. All these promises will be broken. We have got a society that is promoting this mythology that nobody is even going to get a hangnail, no matter how irresponsibly they behave in the financial sector. And it is nonsense. It is a great pandemic delusion, and it is unfortunate because it is ruining the best country in the world."

Analyst Peter Dickmeyer quotes economist Laurence Kotlikoff: "'America's 2018 fiscal gap will come in near $6 trillion, nine times higher than the $666 billion deficit announced by the U.S. Department of the Treasury last week,' says Kotlikoff, an economics professor at Boston University. 'Our country is broke,' says Kotlikoff, who estimates total U.S. government debts at more than $200 trillion, when unfunded liabilities are included. 'We are in worse shape than Russia, China or any developed nation.' According to Kotlikoff, a long-time activist for fiscal rectitude, the problem stems in large part from the fact that the U.S. government has been spending almost all of Americans' approximately $795 billion in social security payroll taxes to pay current bills, rather than investing them to fund retirees' benefits. The upshot is that on a net basis, the U.S. government has no money to pay all the benefits that have been promised."

Financial editor Graham Summers warns, "The Fed and other global central banks are largely being run by academics with zero real world experience. For centuries leaders and their advisors have tried to generate perpetual growth. None have succeeded. So the idea that this current group of central bankers, isolated from the private sector for their entire careers, somehow understand economics better than any other group of humans in history is a ludicrous.

"We don't even have to look back far to see where this ends. A mere 15 years ago, the financial world believed that Alan Greenspan was an economic genius who had brought the world to an era of the New Economy in which we saw non-stop productivity gains. Today we laugh at the ignorance of this. Not content to have created the largest stock bubble in financial history, Greenspan doubled down on his foolishness by creating a housing bubble that was three standard deviations away from historic norms. The fact that he handed off that mess to Ben Bernanke (another ivory tower economist with zero real world experience) before it nearly took down the entire financial system is the greatest accomplishment of his career.

"All told, the bond bubble is now $199 trillion in size. It is over two times the size of global GDP. And because the Fed never bothered to actually crack down on the derivatives markets, there are now $555 trillion in derivatives trading based on bond yields. This is the greatest bubble in history…seven times global GDP and backstopped by nothing more than monetary printing presses."

Author Wolf Richter tells us, "The dizzying borrowing by consumers and businesses that the Fed with its ultra-low interest rates and in its infinite wisdom has purposefully encouraged to fuel economic growth, and to inflate asset prices, has caused debt to pile up. That debt is now eating up cash flows needed for other things, and this is causing pressures, just when interest rates have begun to rise, which will make refinancing this debt more expensive and, for a rising number of consumers and businesses, impossible."

Analyst Egon von Greyerz sums it up, "If global unfunded liabilities of $250 trillion and derivatives of $1.5 quadrillion are included, the world is now staring at total liabilities and risk of $2 quadrillion. When the next crisis starts what central bankers have to focus on is not just global debt but also the derivative bubble. Banks will of course argue that the net derivative figure is much smaller. But in a crisis, gross will remain gross as counter parties fail to settle their obligations. With this background, central bankers must be living on a different planet if they believe they can reduce their balance sheets. Debt in coming years, whether it is government or private debt will go up faster than any time in history.

"When debt defaults start on a bigger scale, central banks will lose control of the interest rates. The manipulation of rates defies all laws of nature and supply and demand. It is not possible to have maximum credit and minimum interest rates. In a free market, if demand for credit is high, the cost of credit will also be very high. When the $280 trillion world debt starts to implode, central banks can no longer hold rates down as the bond markets panic. It will start with the longer rates going up and eventually higher long rates will pull the short rates up.

"As money printing escalates hand-in-hand with defaults, the world will experience hyperinflation on a level that no one can imagine today. At that point debt will probably have grown to tens of quadrillions. Most people will say that it would be impossible for debt to grow to these levels. Anyone who has studied historical debt defaults, money printing and hyperinflation will realize that during these periods, debt grows to many times the original debt. Money printing and hyperinflation become a vicious circle that feeds on itself. Powerless central bankers lose total control and just panic into the next level of money creation. In the end it all fails of course, since printed money can never create wealth. At that point, the hyperinflation turns to a deflationary depression. All credit disappears into a black hole and so does a major part of the financial system. The assets backed by the printed money collapse in value by 90% or more.

"Either we will see a total destruction of paper money in a hyper inflationary scenario or a collapse of the financial system in a deflationary implosion of assets and debts. The most likely in my view is that we will have both. First hyperinflation and then deflation."

How will all of this affect the U.S. currency? According to a leading German banker, Walter Seipp, U.S. dominance of global finance will decline and the U.S. dollar will no longer be the major international currency. He warns, "The U.S. cannot go on as it is at present. The net external debts it would have accumulated…mean that its interest burden would no longer be bearable." He concludes that the dollar will be hard pressed to maintain its position because the currency has, "far more weight than is indicated by the economic and financial significance of the U.S. Its relative decline is fairly certain." Should this happen, and we are suggesting that it could, the price of gold will rise to much higher levels. Not even the mighty U.S. government can borrow, guarantee, and subsidize its way into prosperity. The greater the mortgage placed on our future, the greater the extent of our ultimate decline. The ceiling has not caved in yet, but the cracks are clearly visible to all who wish to see them.

CHAPTER XIV
KILLING THE GOOSE

"Increasingly, the wealth of the modern world has come to be represented by financial assets rather than real assets, and this to me is a very unhealthy situation, because financial assets are inherently unstable. Financial assets (currencies, bonds, mortgages, stocks, bank credit, etc.) can be quickly and violently reduced in value, or destroyed completely by either inflation or deflation."
~ Donald J. Hoppe

Business is hard enough without the difficulties brought on by government interventions. Author Peter Klein gives us further insights. "Ludwig von Mises pointed out, doing business in a world of aggressive governmental regulation is tricky. One consequence is to make firms more bureaucratic, by which Mises means less effective at responding to consumer needs in the most efficient manner. Under capitalism, the size, complexity, and strategy of corporations, reflect the decisions of capitalist-entrepreneurs about how best to earn profit, competing freely with each other for resources and consumer patronage.

"Under interventionism – what we now call crony capitalism – the situation is different. Now companies must employ large staffs of lawyers, accountants, lobbyists, public relations teams, and others who focus not on creating economic value, but on satisfying legal, tax, regulatory, and other government requirements. That large firms are filled with such non-productive employees is not, Mises writes in *Human Action*, a phenomenon of the unhampered market economy,' but a result of government policy.

"In his book *Bureaucracy*, published in 1944, Mises challenges the idea that bureaucracy is a necessary consequence of firm size. 'No profit-seeking enterprise, no matter how large, is liable to become bureaucratic provided the hands of its management are not tied by government interference. The trend toward bureaucratic rigidity is not inherent in the evolution of business. It is an outcome of government meddling with business.'"

Politicians may bark and yap endlessly about the reasons for our economic cycles, but none truly grasp the reasons we have problems. Economic setbacks can't be corrected with a few tax-and-spend measures, subsidies, or meddling in markets. To maintain our economic health we need to cure the following problems:

1. Welfare benefits, unemployment benefits and other subsidy programs weaken the work force. Certain workers will slough off, report late, miss work, or abuse chemicals if they know a government check will replace their paycheck should they be fired. The government provides incentives to goof off.

2. Our low national savings rate is, to some extent, caused by the easy availability of subsidies. People would save more if it weren't for the wide spectrum of programs from cheap loans for education to Social Security. Low savings means we spend more and invest less. Our social safety net helps kill savings.

3. Taxes are a penalty on progress. Federal, state and local taxes can eat up almost half of a worker's earnings. Individuals and corporations could invest this money far more efficiently than the government.

4. The reasons that our industries often lose ground to foreign competition begin with price. They make inroads through underselling us. The main expense of any business is labor. Foreign competition enjoys lower labor costs. Our unions may crow about raising living standards and wages, but they also price companies out of the market and cause job loss.

5. Runaway government spending requires massive borrowing in the capital markets to cover big deficits. This can raise interest rates and crowds out private business. Government sucks up huge amounts of capital that would otherwise be used for constructive economic growth.

6. Business invests enormous energy in complying with a blizzard of laws and regulations. Regulators are a police force

intent on tripping up errant businesses, levying fines or worse. A single regulation can exterminate an entire industry. Too much of management's attention given to regulators detracts from a company's efficiency and profits.

7. Nowadays people sue at the drop of a hat. U.S. business spends too much time and money defending itself against litigation. Suits emanating from the government can paralyze a company for years. Trial lawyers need to be harnessed. America desperately needs tort reform.

8. Government subsidies to certain businesses favor their success against competitors. Legal barriers to starting a business such as permits, bonds, licenses, and regulations help big companies fend off competitors. Government intervention stifles the competition that benefits consumers.

9. Every time the government lays down a new law or changes a regulation, it has the potential for serious damage. Lawmakers and regulators blithely make changes that throw business and industry off the track.

10. The government has fostered a national ethic of getting something for nothing. This burdens business with phony la suits, employee theft, trumped up medical claims, insurance fraud, and an explosion of bad character. For example, generous workers' compensation benefits caused an increase in disability claims for back injuries.

11. Inflation, extreme currency fluctuations, the boom-and-bust cycle, and dollar devaluations, all make doing business more difficult. Inflation tends to make investment in production less rewarding than holding other assets.

12. Business pays for all or part of health insurance, unemployment benefits, workers' compensation insurance, and product liability insurance. When you add legal costs, licensing fees, property taxes, sales tax, income tax, and excise taxes, you have a thoroughbred carrying a 300 pound jockey. In other parts of the world they don't have to carry this much weight.

The government thinks if they take enough money from the people who earn it and subsidize a bunch of people this will somehow create jobs. How dumb are they? Let me tell you what it takes to create jobs. Someone has to turn their back on their financial security, step away from a regular paycheck and risk everything on a business venture. They have to undergo days and nights of racking anxiety, work and struggle for months without gain and skirt the edge of failure while finding the will to persist.

If they can survive this adversity and be creative enough to develop a product or service that people want they can begin to break even and eventually hire someone. That creates one job. No matter how many employees a company eventually has, that's how it starts. Is there anyone in Washington who understands what it takes to create one job?

For every new business that succeeds there are fifty that don't last five years. Those who survive and begin to make a profit are in for a rude awakening. The capital they've managed to earn gets quickly taxed away by the government. This is money that would otherwise be used to create growth and employment. A business strives to gain a financial cushion that will help it survive a slump or downturn. The government takes it away.

The sentiments of most government employees and the multitude who enforce the rules are anti-business. They have little or no knowledge of how the market system works, and they see business as greed-driven, and profits as an evil that government should control. This anti-business attitude proliferates in the media. Both TV and cinema portray business leaders as criminals. The press, magazine, and book publishers are infested with writers expressing a dislike of capitalism. Church leaders reflect these same sentiments. Professors and teachers often sneer at the system that has given them the highest living standard in history.

Economist Richard Ebeling writes, "Why is the free enterprise or capitalist economic system so widely disliked, hated and opposed? Given the success of the competitive market economy to 'deliver the goods,' it presents something of a paradox. One would think that the market economy would be hailed as the most important social institution that humanity had stumbled upon in all of human history. Humanity existed for thousands of years at a level of existence that was at or sometimes even below bare subsistence. The images still shown on our television screens of starving, diseased and seemingly hopeless children in what used to be called 'third world' countries, with appeals for charitable giving to save those young lives, was, in fact, the general condition for the vast majority of human beings everywhere around the globe just a few centuries ago. But such circumstances have been diminishing in a growing number of places in the world. It is not impossible to imagine that before the end of the twenty-first century abject poverty may be a thing of the past. What has made this possible has been a market based economic system. In spite of the astonishing success of market economies in enlarging freedom and prosperity for billions of people, capitalism stands criticized and condemned wherever it exists. Why?"

The French social philosopher Bertrand de Jouvenel (1903-1987) once discussed "The Attitude of the Intellectuals to the Market Economy." First, for them the market economy is "disorderly," that is, they look at the outcomes of the market and assert how much better would be the patterns and relationships and results of society if only there was someone in charge – the government planner, regulator, redistributor – to generate "socially just" outcomes."

These people don't understand wealth creation. They don't understand that profits come from meeting the needs of others by providing products and services that improve living standards. They don't realize that consumers are the rulers of the free market because their buying choices determine the success or failure of the companies competing to serve them. They are unaware that to serve one's self-interest, the capitalist must first serve the self-interest of others. This is the moral underpinning of free enterprise. But rather than notice the unassailable high moral ground of free-market capitalism, they prefer to see greed and inequality.

Economist Thomas Sowell writes, "Think about the things that have improved our lives the most over the past century – medical advances, the transportation revolution, huge increases in consumer goods, dramatic improvements in housing, the computer revolution. The people who created these things – the doers – are not popular heroes. Our heroes are the talkers who complain about the doers."

He continues, "There was a time when most people lived and died within a 50-mile radius of where they were born. The automobile opened a whole new world to these people. It also enabled those living in overcrowded cities to spread out into suburbs and get some elbow room. Trucks got goods to people more cheaply and ambulances got people to hospitals to save their lives. Yet who among the people who did this are today regarded as being as big a hero as Ralph Nader, who put himself on the map with complaints about cars in general and the Corvair in particular? Hard data on automobile safety and tests conducted on the Corvair both undermined Nader's claims. But he will always be a hero to the talkers."

Lew Rockwell points out, "The philosopher who strolls around speculating on the meaning of life is seen as the highest form of humanity, while the man who risks his own money to make available food, shelter, medicine, clothing, and all the other material goods that make life livable is despised."

Animosity towards the merchant class has been around for centuries. Why? The goal of making a profit is quite obviously a self-serving motive. Other occupations, while equally self-serving, are better able to hide their motives. Even though a merchant must provide services for others in order to profit, that part of the equation is overlooked. They're condemned for making a profit.

Lew Rockwell explains how well this profit system works. "It balances human needs with the availability of all the world's resources, unleashes the amazing power of human creativity, and works to meet the material needs of every member of society at the least possible cost. It does this through exchange, cooperation, competition, entrepreneurship, and all the institutions that make possible capitalism – the most productive economic system this side of heaven."

Not long ago I read an article about China and the kind of heroes they glorify in their media. They write about entrepreneurs and business leaders. Contrast that with our hero worship of hip-hop musicians and dysfunctional movie stars. You can read newspaper and magazine articles endlessly about athletes, politicians and entertainers, but not business people (except for a handful, like Martha Stewart, who get into trouble).

These attitudes and policies are killing the goose that laid the golden egg. Without a healthy capitalist economy our spending sins will engulf us. Are we headed towards catastrophe? Author Mark Steyn answers, "In the Western world, countries that were once the crucible of freedom are slipping remorselessly into a thinly disguised serfdom in which an ever higher proportion of your assets are annexed by the state as superlandlord. Big government is where nations go to die – not in Keynes' 'long run,' but sooner than you think."

I'm dismayed by the current level of hatred directed towards capitalism. In my lifetime I've never heard such expressions of bitterness. This is the consequence of left-wing professors and the liberal media poisoning the well. Liberal parents have managed to turn their offspring into good little Marxists or at least into people who share Marxist animosity towards free markets and capitalism. They grossly exaggerate the so-called sins of capitalism and believe any canard no matter how baseless.

Author James Bovard writes, "In a New York Times tribune headline, 'Happy Birthday, Karl Marx. You Were Right.' Philosophy professor Jason Barker declared that 'educated liberal opinion is today more or less unanimous in its agreement with Marx's basic thesis' that capitalism is fatally flawed."

What is it with today's liberals mouthing Marxist platitudes and anti-capitalist drivel? They are the worst mealy-mouthed do-gooders in history. Their bumbling, exorbitantly expensive attempts at social justice have had a ruinous impact on the recipients of subsidies. Their constant engineering of higher taxes and easy money has harmed the economy. Their regulators have convoluted markets and put their energy fads ahead of practical solutions. On top of these colossal failures they have the nerve to condemn capitalism.

CHAPTER XV
THE KEYNESIAN FALLACY

"There can be no other criterion, no other standard than gold. Yes, gold which never changes, which can be shaped into ingots, bars, coins, which has no nationality and which is eternally and universally accepted as the unalterable fiduciary value par excellence."

~ Charles de Gaulle

Here's a quote from PayPal founder Peter Thiel's excellent book *Zero to One*: "If you can identify a delusional popular belief, you can find what lies behind it: the contrarian truth." We are confronted daily with the greatest economic and financial delusion of all time: Keynesian economics. The contrarian truth behind Keynesianism is that it must fail. Government is the greatest advocate of Keynesian economics because it finances government spending. The socialism that's paid for by Keynesian money creation has never worked in history, but has engineered economic and social suffering on a scale so enormous we can't comprehend it.

Besides socialism, the other great beneficiary of Keynesian policies is Wall Street and its minions who see no harm as long as stocks finish up. They care not about the loss to the public's savings or the income disparity that inflation creates. These shallowest of thinkers ignore the speculative excess and the inevitable boom and bust to worship at the altar of the Fed. They fail to understand that the money printing they swoon over is the favored method of financing the welfare state and socialism.

The essence of Keynesianism in America is money creation and inflation. In his book *The Ethics of Money Production*, the Austrian economist Jörg Hülsmann described inflation's cultural and spiritual legacy: "The notion that inflation is harmful is a staple of economic science. To appreciate the disruptive nature of inflation in its full extent we must keep in mind that it springs from a violation of the fundamental rules of society. Inflation is what happens when people increase the money supply by fraud, imposition, and breach of contract. Invariably it produces three characteristic consequences: (1) it benefits the perpetrators at the expense of all other money users; (2) it allows the accumulation of debt beyond the level debts could reach on the free market; and (3) it reduces the purchasing power of money below the level it would have reached on the free market.

"While these three consequences are bad enough, things get much worse once inflation is encouraged and promoted by the state. The government's fiat makes inflation perennial, and as a result we observe the formation of inflation-specific institutions and habits. Thus fiat inflation leaves a characteristic cultural and spiritual stain on human society."

More important for the short term are the economic consequences which include the possible destruction of the dollar through hyper-inflation. This likely outcome is brought on by our ongoing monetization of the debt. You cannot pay a nation's bills forever by printing or creating new money. The markets will eventually enforce repercussions. No money in history has withstood permanent inflating. In fact, all paper, fiat currencies eventually become worthless for the same reason.

No one ever explained the damage that inflation does like the great libertarian writer for Newsweek and the New York Times, Henry Hazlitt (1894-1993). He wrote, "When the Federal Reserve banks buy government notes or bonds in the open market, they pay for them, directly or indirectly, by creating money. This is what is known as 'monetizing' the public debt. Inflation goes on as long as this goes on." The consequences are dire indeed. "Inflation must always end in a crisis and a slump, and worse than the slump itself may be the public delusion that the slump has been caused, not by the previous inflating, but by the inherent defects of a free market."

Hazlitt warned, "It is harmful because it depreciates the value of the monetary unit, raises everybody's cost of living, imposes what is in effect a tax on the poorest…wipes out the value of past savings, discourages future savings, redistributes wealth and income wantonly, encourages and rewards speculation and gambling at the expense of thrift and work, undermines confidence in the justice of a free enterprise system, and corrupts public and private morals."

He continued, "A period of inflation is almost inevitably also a period when demagogy and anti-business mentality are rampant. If implacable enemies of the country had deliberately set out to undermine and destroy the incentives of the middle classes to work and save, they could hardly have contrived a more effective set of weapons than the present combination of inflation, subsidies, handouts, and confiscatory taxes that our own politicians have imposed upon us."

Mr. Hazlitt explained further, "In a free enterprise system, with an honest and stable money, there is dominantly a close link between effort and productivity on the one hand, and economic reward on the other. Inflation severs this link. Reward comes to depend less and less on effort and production, and more and more on successful gambling and luck."

He continued his litany of warnings: "It is not merely that inflation breeds dishonesty in a nation. Inflation is itself a dishonest act on the part of government, and sets the example for private citizens. When modern governments inflate by increasing the paper money supply, directly or indirectly, they do in principle what kings once did when they clipped coins. Diluting the money supply with paper is the moral equivalent of diluting the milk supply with water. Notwithstanding all the pious pretenses of governments that inflation is some evil visitation from without, inflation is practically always the result of deliberate governmental policy."

Government and its inflationary policies had no greater enemy than the Austrian School economist Murray Rothbard (1926-1995). He wrote, "The natural tendency of government, once in charge of money, is to inflate and to destroy the value of the currency. To understand this truth we must examine the nature of government and of the creation of money. Throughout history, governments have been chronically short of revenue. The reason should be clear: unlike you and I, governments do not produce useful goods and services which they can sell on the market; governments, rather than producing and selling services, live parasitically off the market and off society. Unlike every other person and institution in society, government obtains its revenue from coercion, from taxation.

"If taxation is permanently short of the style of expenditures desired by the State, how can it make up the difference? By getting control of the money supply, or, to put it bluntly, by counterfeiting. Indeed, the best way to penetrate the mysteries of the modern monetary and banking system is to realize that the government and its central bank act precisely as would a Grand Counterfeiter, with very similar social and economic effects."

Two decades ago I became friends with an economist by the name of John King. He had written a book stressing the likelihood of deflation. Since I occasionally talked on the phone with Murray Rothbard who was then the Distinguished Professor of Economics at the University of Nevada, Las Vegas, I decided to send him John King's book for his opinion. I chuckle to this day over his letter of response which dismissed the book as "a veritable tissue of error."

A much greater threat than deflation according to Professor Rothbard was the possibility of hyperinflation. "As inflation proceeds, people begin to realize that prices are going up perpetually as a result of perpetual inflation. Now people will say: 'I will buy now, though prices are high, because if I wait, prices will go up still further.' As a result, the demand for money now falls and prices go up more, proportionately, than the increase in the money supply. At this point, the government is often called upon to 'relieve the money shortage' caused by the accelerated price rise, and it inflates even faster. Soon, the country reaches the state of the 'crack-up boom,' when people say: 'I must buy anything now – anything to get rid of money which depreciates in my hands.' The supply of money skyrockets, the demand plummets, and prices rise astronomically. The monetary system has, in effect, broken down completely, and the economy reverts to other moneys, if they are attainable – other metal, foreign currencies if this is a one-country inflation, or even a return to barter conditions…. The monetary system has broken down under the impact of inflation."

In 1931 Mr. Bresciani-Turroni wrote of the Weimar inflation in Germany, "It annihilated thrift…it destroyed incalculable moral and intellectual values. It provoked a serious revolution in social classes, a few people accumulating wealth and forming a class of usurpers of national property, whilst millions of individuals were thrown into poverty. It was a distressing preoccupation and constant torment of innumerable families; it poisoned the German people by spreading among all classes the spirit of speculation and by diverting them from proper and regular work, and it was the cause of incessant political and moral disturbances." That was in 1931, before the hell that followed.

In 1876 Andrew Dickson White wrote of the great French inflation of the 1790's, "With prices soaring and the value of money savings rapidly diminishing, an early effect was the obliteration of thrift. Accompanying this was a cancerous increase in speculation and gambling. Stock-jobbing became rife. More and more people began to see the advantages of borrowing and later paying off in depreciated money. A great debtor class grew up whose interest was to keep the inflation going. Workers, finding themselves with less and less real pay in terms of what their wages would buy, while others grew rich by gambling, began to lose interest in steady work. The evaporation of the incomes and savings of the lower and middle classes, and the sudden enrichment of speculators, with their ostentatious luxury, led to mounting social resentment and unrest."

Periods of inflation in the modern era are often interspersed with periods of deflation. That's because money and credit creation generate a boom in the economy which ultimately leads to a bust. Sometimes the newly created money fails to stoke a booming economy, but flows into assets. When stocks and real estate increase dramatically in a period of easy money, that is asset inflation. A period of deflation can lead to bear markets and declining asset values.

CHAPTER XVI
BLAMELESS

"Betting against gold is the same as betting on governments. He who bets on governments and government money bets against 6,000 years of recorded human history."
~ Gary North

In the market economy a business must serve others in a beneficial way in order to succeed. That is the beauty of capitalism. In order to profit, you must make your customers' lives better. It's a form of the Golden Rule. This is what the liberal wing of the Democratic Party refuses to understand. The necessity to serve others in order to profit means that free market capitalism holds the moral high ground. Under socialism, no similar requirement exists. Instead of consumers having the free choice of goods and services, they are provided for by government dictate. Whenever that has been tried it has deprived consumers and made them poorer. Nothing can compare with the bounty and product options of capitalism. In the entire history of socialism it has not been able to create a single commercial innovation. Meanwhile, capitalism has showered us with so many material blessings we can't keep track of them. Free markets have eliminated starvation, disease and great swaths of poverty.

Capitalism creates wealth, opportunities, work and success. Austrian economist Ludwig von Mises wrote this about capitalism, "If you seek its monument look around you." In other words, the blessings of capitalism are all around us every day in every way. Henry Hazlitt reminds us, "Modern capitalism benefited the masses in a double way – both by greatly increasing the wages of the masses of workers and greatly reducing the real prices they had to pay for what was produced."

You can only have true freedom under the market economy. The consumers are kings and queens in the market economy. Their buying decisions determine what companies succeed or fail. Heavy-handed interference by the government means a reduction of buying choices. That's another way of saying reduced freedoms. A business owner's motives may well be selfish but the consumers are merciless and a business must serve them well or perish. It's as near to a perfect system as humanity will ever achieve.

Entrepreneurs like Steve Jobs and Bill Gates operating within the market system changed our lives. Despite all this evidence liberals and socialists continue to denigrate the free market. They argue for redistribution, high taxes and more government control. They disdain capitalism. They cannot see the benefits of a free market because their core beliefs are false. Many of them see evil existing in the market economy. They are harbingers of backwardness and poverty.

We hear them chatter incessantly about income inequality. They push the idea that the market system bears responsibility for the rich getting richer while the middle class suffers. In reality it is their socialist schemes and intrusions into the market that hurt us. For example, pumping out money and credit causes asset inflation that rewards the owners of stocks, bonds, real estate, farmland, art and antiques. The middle class who don't own these assets miss out. Liberals promote big government despite its detrimental impact on our economy. Look at what these liberals have saddled us with. Start with unions. The left passed laws that allowed unions to get a stranglehold on major industries. At one time our automakers dominated world markets. By 1980 Japanese cars had replaced U.S. cars the world over. Union work rules, lush benefits, and impossibly high wages for unskilled workers made it easy for the competition to overtake us.

The larger profits are, the more wealth the entrepreneur has created for others, and indeed, the largest profits accrue to those firms that have supplied the most valuable goods and services to the masses. How perverse that this precious talent for raising the standards of living of others induces those resentful souls on the left to paint a bull's-eye on the back of those wealth creators and make them targets for the government to confiscate more of the profits they justly earned in service to others.

Columnist Vasco Kohlmayer writes, "Capitalism is increasingly cast as the great villain of our time. It's blamed for exploitation, poverty, fraud, alienation, crime, racism and nearly everything else. The bad rap could not be more undeserved. Rather than mankind's scourge, capitalism has been its greatest benefactor. It is, in fact, the only socio-economic system that can provide ordinary people with dignified and prosperous lives. It was only with the advent of capitalism that the common man was able to escape the penury and filth of his existence to which he had been previously consigned. Until then, the lives of most people were short, hard and miserable. Today, as if by miracle, we can enjoy greater comforts and ease of life than the kings of the past."

Author Lew Rockwell confirms, "Capitalism, and capitalism alone, has rescued the human race from degrading poverty, rampant sickness and early death." Kohlmayer points out, "Capitalism is responsible for nearly everything that makes human existence easy and comfortable. The automobile, the supermarket, the personal computer, the washing machine, the hammer-drill, the iPhone, the airplane, the TV set, the chewing gum, electricity and countless other good things have all been birthed and mass-produced by capitalism."

Rockwell agrees. "The profit system balances human needs with the availability of all the world's resources, unleashes the amazing power of human creativity, and works to meet the material needs of every member of society at the least possible cost. It does this through exchange, cooperation, competition, entrepreneurship, and all the institutions that make possible capitalism – the most productive economic system this side of heaven."

Says Kohlmayer, "Because of its immense wealth-generating power, people who live in capitalist societies enjoy rising standards of living and material affluence. Conversely, those who live in non-capitalist societies invariably experience the opposite…. The rule always holds: Capitalist societies are invariably prosperous. Non-capitalist ones are always poor." Columnist Walter Williams sums it up; "Notwithstanding all of the demagoguery, it is capitalism not socialism that made us a great country and it's socialism that will be our undoing."

George Gilder writes, "The most important question for the future of America is how we treat our entrepreneurs. If our government continues to smear, harass, overtax, and oppressively regulate them, we will be dismayed by how swiftly the engines of American prosperity deteriorate. We will be amazed at how quickly American wealth flees to other countries."

The profit-seeking entrepreneur – not any government, church, charity or other worthy entity – deserves the credit for lifting us out of poverty and creating our material abundance. We should be grateful for entrepreneurs. They are our economic benefactors, the wealth creators who have enriched our lives. They stand as testimony to the wealth-creating superiority of capitalism.

Recently my wife and I had dinner with an architect we hired to remodel our house. Over dinner we began a mild political discussion. One of the arguments he made was something you hear a lot. He claimed that labor unions (in the early 20th century) were responsible for raising the wages of the working man and eliminating child labor. According to him unions had raised our living standards.

None of that is true. Capitalism and capitalism alone was responsible for raising wages. When workers began to prosper and make enough money their children no longer had to work. Prior to capitalism many children had to labor or face starvation. In most parts of the world capitalism eliminated starvation. Prosperity and improved living standards came from capital investment, free markets, entrepreneurship, low taxes and minimal government intervention. When labor unions disrupted capitalism they were an impediment to prosperity.

A recently published book promotes the idea that government was primarily responsible for the growth and prosperity of the middle class following the Second World War. However, it wasn't the government that brought us television, jet engines, air conditioning, lasers, computers and the polio vaccine. And it wasn't capitalism that brought us rising crime rates, failing schools, worsening poverty, high inflation and rising taxes. All anyone needs to do to verify the effectiveness of capitalism is to look around and see the products that improve their life.

People who vote for the opponents of capitalism often say, "I'm not against capitalism." Yet they support those who cripple capitalism with government intervention and who milk the capitalists dry with taxes. There is no middle road between a government-managed economy and a capitalist economy. There is only less and less capitalism. The people who want to regulate and oversee capitalism have no conception of how much they are damaging capitalism and with it America's economic greatness and prosperity.

The money that comes out of Washington to fund liberal giveaways has changed the financial landscape in and around our capital. A recent article from Forbes listed the wealthiest 24 counties in America. Not surprisingly 12 of the 24 were in Virginia and Maryland clustered around Washington D. C. When taxes are sent to Washington to be passed out to favorite constituencies a lot of it greases the locals. Consulting firms, sub-contractors and others are funded first for so-called equitable outcomes and then for the job to be done. Furthermore, every big corporation or interest group has to open an office or hire a lawyer or lobbyist to secure special favors or keep the government from ruining them. Then you have a growing army of government workers. A federal employee now earns on average about twice what private sector employees get. Then there are the fat retirement benefits for government workers, many who retire at age 50.

CHAPTER XVII
FREEDOM PHILOSOPHER

"The proper and limited use of government is to invoke a common justice and keep the peace - and that is all."

~ Leonard Read

If Ludwig von Mises gave body to the economics of freedom, then his friend and contemporary, Leonard Read gave it spirit. Leonard Read (1898-1983) founded the Foundation for Economic Education. He wrote 29 books. In his biography, Mary Sennholz wrote that he "...rallied the demoralized and tired forces of individual freedom..."

Writing in 1946, Leonard Read warned about the inroads of government: "More and more people are coming to believe that the free market should be shelved and that, in its stead, government should use its police force to take the income of some and give it...to the government's idea of the needy." In other words, from each according to his effort, to each according to his lack of effort.

A half-century ago Read could write, "Socialistic practices are now so ingrained in our thinking, so customary, so much a part of our mores, that we take them for granted." Today's scope and size of public housing, Medicare and government subsidies dwarfs anything in Leonard Read's time. He, I'm sure, would argue that we have embraced socialism all the more.

One sign of the damaging effect of these subsidies shows up in elections. Joseph Sobran aptly describes the reason liberals win. "Voters who live off taxpayers are the Democrats' ace in the hole. The Democrats created the big programs and never let the recipients forget it. This gives them an initial advantage of tens of millions of votes in any presidential election."

Leonard Read held these vote-buying government programs in contempt. He wrote, "Statism is but socialized dishonesty; it is feathering the nests of some with feathers coercively plucked from others

– on the grand scale. There is no moral difference between the act of a pickpocket and the progressive income tax or any other social program." He explained, "There is no greater dishonesty than man effecting his own private gains at the expense of others...the practice of dishonesty is evil and...retribution follows the doing of evil. Every evil act commits us to its retribution."

Leonard Read asks, "Is the extortion of your income (in order that another may have the say-so as to what it will be spent for) a creative act?" His answer: "Extortion – coercion – is destructive. It destroys your freedom of choice! Coercion, by its nature, is destructive." (In this context coercion means forcing a citizen to do what he or she would not do if left to their own devices.) He quotes Frederic Bastiat as the litmus test on whether a government action is aggressive or violent. "See if the law takes from some persons what belongs to them, and gives it to other persons to whom it does not belong."

Because of government coercion a trickle of people are beginning to leave the U.S. Some leave to escape the high taxes. Others resent the degree of government intrusion. These libertarians are searching the world over for comfortable climates, amenities and maximum freedom. Others consider leaving because they are horrified by the results of government programs that foster crime and bad character. They look for crime-free zones within and outside the U.S.

Towards the end of the Roman Empire its citizens began to leave Rome (300 AD). It was the only way to escape exorbitant taxes, mobs of poor clamoring for government handouts and heavy-handed bureaucrats strangling private business. We haven't quite come to that yet, but present trends of redistribution ultimately spell disaster. The policies of the liberals and socialists are the prescription for national suicide.

Leonard Read argued that income redistribution harms everyone involved in the process, starting with the person whose property or assets are taken. It discourages private charity, "that kindly sentiment and conduct which strengthens the bonds of a common brotherhood." Read saw voluntary charity as a highly important attribute of society and decried its decline. He complained, "The state will practice charity for you. A common brotherhood, by some quirk of reasoning, is to become a collective act of compulsion!" He also saw enormous economic damage. Savings (now taxed off) would otherwise have been invested in tools, machinery and factories to create jobs, wealth and greater financial security.

Of the person in need Leonard Read writes, "Does any able adult person 'in need' really benefit by living on the confiscated income of others? Does this ever improve his character or his mental and physical faculties? His growth? Does anyone ever benefit by the removal of self-responsibility?" He adds "To live on loot appears to be no further removed from evil than to take the loot." It should be plain to see "that the evil means of confiscating income must lead to an evil end to those who live on it."

Of the bureaucrats who tax and enforce Leonard Read wrote, "I cannot indulge in my own upgrading at the same time I am inhibiting someone else's creative action. Therefore, to the extent that one's life is spent in using force to coerce others, to that extent is one's life destroyed and its higher purpose frustrated."

Leonard Read knew that the absence of government intrusion was responsible for the great burst of creativity that lifted our country to its exalted economic position. He wrote, "The Constitution and the Bill of Rights more severely limited government than government had ever before been limited." Two benefits occurred. "...individuals did not turn to government for security, welfare, or prosperity because government was so limited that it had little on hand to dispense..." and this limited power did not "permit taking from some citizens and giving to others."

So, "The American people gained a world-wide reputation for being self-reliant." And since the government did not much interfere, tax away income or force people to do what they otherwise wouldn't do, "there was a freeing, a releasing of creative energy on a scale unheard of before." Excessive government (socialism) intimidates and discourages this process. Says Read, "Nothing creative is induced by compulsion." In other words, "Law and decree cannot serve as a creative force, any more than can a gun."

The Soviets showed us how sterile and destructive to human creativity is socialism. They survived on what they stole, borrowed or copied because socialism "depends upon…material achievements which socialism itself can never create." This is the definition of a parasite. "Socialism takes and redistributes wealth, but it is utterly incapable of creating wealth." In other words, social programs detract from our prosperity.

Leonard Read further warned, "Man cannot feign the role of God without finally playing the devil's part." Is there any better example of this than in the socialist Russia of Lenin and Stalin? Through the horrible deeds and consequences of collectivist actions we can see clearly "that man playing God is a prime evil, an evil seed that must grow to a destructive bloom, however pretty it may appear in its earlier stages."

Read wrote, "We cannot maintain the present degree of statism, let alone drive further toward the omnipotent state, without our great economy flying to pieces." He warned of this peril decades ago. Yet he has passed from the scene and no serious collapse occurred. Why then haven't we seen a crash? How have we avoided a crisis? The answer: inflation. We take larger and larger doses of financial narcotics to forestall pain.

Inflation means diluting the dollar's purchasing power through increasing the money supply. Why do we do this? Says Read, "Inflation makes the extension of socialism possible by providing the financial chaos in which it flourishes. The fact is that socialism and inflation are simultaneously cause and effect; they feed on each other!"

Inflation also keeps the financial markets rising. New money funnels into speculation, leveraging, borrowing and refinancing. It lubricates a vast credit and debt expansion, encouraging consumers to borrow to the hilt, thereby feeding a consumption boom that keeps the economy humming. Inflating provides short-term bliss while monstrous balance-of-payment deficits, reliance on foreign lenders, low capital formation, meager savings, faltering productivity, and high levels of public and private debt chronicle the insidious works of socialism.

Socialism kills progress, destroys creativity, reduces freedom, chokes off productivity and bleeds the citizens dry. It bankrupts nations. It has hidden its sorry results by lurking behind mountains of debt and by slowly ruining the currency through inflation. When its dirty work is finally complete, the economy will be ruined, the markets in a shambles, the currency debased and the people in shock. A wise man said, "Ultimately with God's aid, Truth always emerges and finally prevails supreme in its power over the destiny of mankind, and terrible is the retribution for those who deny, defy, or betray it."

This crash I write about will not be postponed indefinitely. The single best historic indicator of economic collapse and shrinking prosperity has been unprecedented extremes in debt, speculation, consumption, leverage, stock values and social trends. It is these excesses that can turn normal corrections into panics because the margins for error have been eroded by excessive optimism, and arrogance. The refusal to see the enormity of the current excesses and to ignore the sorry historical record of panics and crashes is in itself a sign of trouble ahead. It's quite possible that this nearsighted nation stands on the precipice of a historic collapse.

CHAPTER XVIII

ENVY

"Social justice rests on the hate towards those that enjoy a comfortable position, namely, upon envy."
~ Friedrich Hayek

I have these two acquaintances who are big believers in high taxes and heavy government regulation. One is a lawyer who did OK in his career but never made a lot of money. The other was in real estate and after years of disappointing results retired with modest means. They are both envious of people who made a lot of money. Envy is what makes them liberals.

Scratch a leftist and you'll find a person who's worried about someone else making a profit or high income. Why is that? Envy explains these sentiments. Author Helmut Schoek writes, "Envy is a drive which lies at the core of man's life as a social being..." In America the politics of envy can get you elected to the highest office in the land.

Under capitalism, everyone has the opportunity to become an entrepreneur or attain a profession or position that pays off handsomely. However, this system allows no excuses for personal shortcomings or failures. Many self-made people started from the same place as others who failed or who did not forge ahead. The sight of people who have given proof of greater ability bothers some people. To console themselves they rationalize that their skills have gone unrecognized. They blame capitalism, which they claim does not reward the meritorious but gives the prize to dishonest businesses, and other exploiters. They were too honest to swindle people, and they chose virtue over riches.

In a society where everyone is the founder of his or her own fortune, it is particularly galling to the teacher, the politician, the artist or the bureaucrat to see the large income disparity between themselves and successful entrepreneurs. Their envy turns them to socialism, which promises to level incomes and allows the state to control economic outcomes.

The Austrian economist Ludwig von Mises put it this way: "Envy is a widespread frailty. It is certain that many intellectuals envy the higher income of prosperous businessmen and that these feelings drive them toward socialism. They believe that the authorities of a socialist commonwealth would pay them higher salaries than those that they earn under capitalism."

Mises further argued, "What pushes the masses into the camp of socialism is even more than the illusion that socialism will make them richer, the expectation that it will curb all those who are better than they themselves are…"

Even among some conservatives there exists an unhealthy level of envy toward the wealthy. They join with professors and politicians to suggest that the worst exploitation and greed comes from big business. They fail to realize that large corporations got that way because they did a superior job of meeting the product needs of the people in the best, most economical way.

The hallmark of big business is mass production for the benefit of the masses. In fact, big business standardizes the people's ways of consumption and enjoyment, and every citizen shares in most of these material blessings.

Nobody goes without in the market economy because someone got rich. The same process that makes people rich satisfies people's wants and needs. The most millionaires are found in countries with the highest living standards. The entrepreneurs and the capitalists prosper only to the extent that they succeed in supplying and satisfying the consumer.

The glaring misunderstanding of capitalism and how it works in our society originates more from envy than intellect. This mix of envy and ignorance explains everything from the inroads of Lenin to the socialists who have led us down the path to fewer freedoms and more government. The liberals in our government promote a detrimental socialist philosophy.

Lew Rockwell runs the Ludwig von Mises Institute in Auburn, Alabama. His excellent book, *Speaking of Liberty*, explains why so much hostility exists towards business. "Whether in the arts, entertainment, or academia, the dominant players are talented people who believe that they are wiser and better than the masses. They are appalled that capitalism permits a B-school dropout to become a billionaire while they scrape by for a measly raise when promoted from assistant to associate professor. They set out to cripple the system that brings this about."

And what does this envy lead to? Rockwell continues, "Outside of one or two economics professors, nearly the entire liberal arts faculty of the typical university is reliably anti-capitalist. As a class, liberal arts academics can be depended on to oppose economic development, support high taxes, and latch on to every anti-enterprise cause that comes along." Philosopher Andrew J. Galambos sumps it up, "The cheap but simple human emotion of envy is the driving force of all socialism, of all anti-capitalist philosophy. It is the mark of the intellectual."

Envy on the left expresses itself in their constant demands for higher taxes. There's a generally held belief that an upward limit exists on how high taxes can be raised. If taxes go too high, there's no question it damages the economy. However, that will not persuade the left wing or their political candidates to forgo tax increases. Envious liberals refuse to see that high taxes hurt economic progress. They listen to left-leaning claims that higher taxes will make little or no difference to the economy.

For the most part leftists don't care about consequences as long as their precious social programs get funded. And, if some rich folks get the shaft, it's all the more fun. The deep vein of envy on the left means it wouldn't bother them a bit to see taxes on the wealthy go to 90% with strict limits on what people can earn and what they can own. They are currently advocating excess profits taxes, raising the income tax, hiking the capital gains tax, increasing state income taxes, sales taxes and corporate taxes.

Once liberals get into power, social costs will rise precipitously and taxes will become punitive. Most leftists would secretly like to become Lenin. Since they share his view that wealth and success are only a matter of luck, it wouldn't bother them to strip the affluent of every penny. Author Neal Boortz writes, "If the Liberal Left can create the common perception that success and failure are simple matters of 'fortune' or 'luck,' then it is easy to promote and justify their various income redistribution schemes."

Author James Bovard reminds us, "Government aid programs have been endlessly expanded, and the government has sought to maximize the number of people willing to accept handouts…. Roughly half of all Americans are dependent on the government, either for handouts, pensions, or paychecks…. There are more than 20 million government employees in the United States – more than the total number of Americans employed in manufacturing…. The sheer number of government employees and welfare recipients effectively transforms the purpose of government from maintaining order to confiscating as much as possible from vulnerable taxpayers…. Once a person becomes a government dependent, his moral standing to resist the expansion of government power is fatally compromised."

There's a lot at stake in coming elections. If the redistributors and their subsidized followers win out, America's waning greatness will fade away for good. The downside is a nightmare. It's the road to hyperinflation, depression, dollar destruction, national decline and insolvency. Ludwig von Mises instructed, "No one can find a safe way out for himself if society is sweeping towards destruction. Therefore everyone, in his own interests, must thrust himself vigorously into the intellectual battle. None can stand aside with unconcern; the interests of everyone hang on the result. Whether he chooses or not, every man is drawn into the great historical struggle, the decisive battle into which our epoch has plunged us."

Mises concludes, "Our whole civilization rests on the fact that men have always succeeded in beating off the attack of the redistributors."

CHAPTER XIX
HERO TO THE LEFT

"Since the 8th century in China, hundreds of fiat-money monetary systems have been attempted. And 100% of the time, they have failed. Why should a monetary system, that hasn't worked for 1,200 years, suddenly work now?"

~ Lawrence M. Parks

For the most part, liberals in America take their economic cues from New York Times columnist Paul Krugman. From his post at the Times the Keynesian Krugman promotes socialized health care, increased welfare payments, higher taxes, and massive government spending. The far left in this country has limited economic insight on the origins of prosperity. You really have to wonder about Mr. Krugman when he writes that capitalism is inhumane and the free market is amoral. It escapes him that wherever it has been practiced, capitalism eliminated starvation, rolled back disease and dramatically improved living standards. As economist Lewellyn Rockwell puts it, "The market economy has created unfathomable prosperity and, decade-by-decade, century-by-century, miraculous feats of innovation, production, distribution, and social coordination. To the free market, we owe all material prosperity, all leisure time, our health and longevity, our huge and growing population and nearly everything we call life itself."

I'm afraid most of the Keynesians running our country don't have any more understanding about wealth creation than does Mr. Krugman when he writes, "Nobody really knows why the U.S. economy could generate 3 percent annual productivity growth before 1973 and only 1 percent afterward; nobody really knows why Japan surged from defeat to global economic power after World War II, while Britain slid slowly into third-rate status." Believe it or not, they don't know that low taxes, less regulation, sound money, high savings and a market economy will cause rapid growth. Rather, they see injustice because everybody's economic outcomes are not the same. It drives them crazy that they don't get the same share as successful entrepreneurs.

We are in real danger when an influential, Nobel Prize-winning liberal economist can write that we "don't know how to make a poor country rich or bring back the magic of economic growth when it seems to have gone away." It's certainly true that the liberals in Washington don't know how to invigorate our economy. In fact, if the politicians follow Mr. Krugman's advice, we can throw in the towel on the economy. Fortunately, the Republicans got us some tax relief and the economy responded.

It's not that hard. Adam Smith summed it up. "Little else is required to carry a state to the highest degree of opulence from the lowest barbarism, but peace, easy taxes and a tolerable administration of justice." Or how about Ben Franklin: "In short, the way to wealth, if you desire it, is as plain as the way to market. It depends chiefly on two words, industry and frugality." Economist Ludwig von Mises sums up what Keynesians and liberals never seem to understand regarding the need for savings. "A country becomes more prosperous in proportion to the rise in the invested capital per unit of its population."

The reason that liberalism is so dangerous to America is that they never learn from their failures (welfarism) or from the successes of capitalism. Newsletter editor Bill Buckler writes about one such triumph. "In the aftermath of WW II, large parts of Germany were little more than piles of rubble or smoking ashes. Most of their major cities had been all but destroyed by bombing. Their infrastructure and transportation links lay in ruins. The nation itself was fully occupied by the conquering powers and in the process of being split in half with the eastern half swallowed by USSR-sponsored totalitarianism.

"The Germans themselves were utterly demoralized, having lost a world war for the second time in one generation. What economic exchange there was took place by means of barter. Cigarettes were used as money for those who had no access to the 'scrip' issued by the occupying powers.... 'Aid' did not resuscitate the western half of Germany – a return to sound economics and (relatively) sound money did.

"The process was simplicity itself. In one move over a long weekend in mid-1948, the German government...[abolished] controls on prices and wages and [lifted] most of the regulatory structure on the economy.... The next day, the German people almost literally began to construct a new nation out of the rubble. Inside of a decade, Germany had one of the most dynamic and richest economies in the world and a currency which was arguably the soundest in the world.

"In the words of the great Austrian Economist, Wilhelm Roepke, advisor to German Economics Minister Ludwig Erhard at the time: "...here is to be found the most convincing case in all history against collectivism and inflationism and for market economy and monetary discipline."

Rather than adopt the free market economic policies that have time and again proven their merit, Paul Krugman espouses socialistic schemes that have never worked. As Winston Churchill once quipped, "The inherent vice of capitalism is the unequal sharing of blessings; the inherent virtue of socialism is the equal sharing of misery."

The essence of our contemporary application of Keynesian economics is best described by analyst Michael Metrosky. "Spend all the money you have. When you run out of money, borrow all you can and spend that too. When nobody will loan you any more money, just print the money and keep spending." It's a fitting epitaph for an economy in the process of being killed by the likes of Mr. Krugman, the New York Times and the Keynesians in Washington who have been in charge over the past many administrations.

Nobody gets under the skin of conservatives and libertarians like Paul Krugman. Lately he's sunk to a new low by claiming that the underlying motivation for conservative views is racial. He wrote, "Race is the Rosetta Stone that makes sense...of U.S. politics." He claims that conservative politics is driven by the belief that the government is taking their hard-earned money to give to minorities.

Arguments like this further drive a wedge between the races and the two political parties. It's more than divisive, it's hateful. The reality is that conservatives want to see minorities succeed. For the most part they bend over backwards to help people. Conservatives are known to be far more charitable than liberals. They are not in the least threatened by the success of anyone.

However, conservatives do understand one exceedingly important thing. People must make their own way in life. The helping hand of the government is too often a push backwards. When permanent subsidies began to replace private charity, the circumstances of the poor took a turn for the worse and their condition continues to deteriorate to this day.

Nothing differentiates the views of the left and right like this sentence by Mr. Krugman: "The reason so many Americans remain trapped in poverty isn't that the government helps them too much; it's that it helps them too little." The trillions spent on social welfare have left wide swaths of people unemployable and unable to fend for themselves. Crime and addiction have worsened. Unwed mothers and irresponsible parents have doomed untold numbers of children to the criminal justice system. Underprivileged people were far more upright a century ago, before subsidies.

The failure to see the cause of society's disintegration and the threat it poses for America makes Mr. Krugman's errors the modern equivalent of a belief in human sacrifice. Furthermore, his Keynesian economic theories have caused inflation and recessions. In fact, he recommended the creation of a housing bubble prior to the housing collapse that caused untold pain for homeowners. His endorsement of deficit spending, excessive regulation and exorbitant taxes are policies that have hamstrung the economy. Nevertheless, he does the thinking for a vast contingent of liberals from his influential post at the Times.

Many on the left are in awe of Nobel Prize-winning Krugman. However, when you read some of the things he has written the genius label is laughable. Here's what Krugman said about the internet and technology back in 1998: "The growth of the internet will slow drastically, as the flaw in 'Metcalfe's law,' which states that the number of potential connections in a network is proportional to the square of the number of participants, becomes apparent: most people have nothing to say to each other! By 2005 or so, it will become clear that the internet's impact on the economy has been no greater than the fax machine.... As the rate of technological change in computing slows, the number of jobs for IT specialists will decelerate, then actually turn down; ten years from now, the phrase 'information economy' will sound silly."

CHAPTER XX

INFLATION

"Individuals should hold gold as a true diversification and hedge against the credit bubble bursting. This is why intelligent people have held gold for generations."

~ David Tice

M ost people are oblivious to what's going on in America. They don't "get it." You may not either. If so, I'm going to give it to you straight. It's time for a wake-up call. It's time for you to "get it." If you don't "get it," your financial future is dim.

Several years ago I was talking with my 72-year old corporate counsel, who is planning to retire. I told him he couldn't afford to retire. "You only have a million dollars," I said. "Subtract a $100,000 a year for inflation. In nine years you have the purchasing power of $100,000. You'll be greeting people at Wal-Mart." I was only guessing about his net worth. Perhaps he's got $2 million or more. I continued, "You've got guys managing your money who don't "get it." You've got these establishment guys with conventional investments in stocks and bonds, and they don't see the big picture. They could wipe you out." "I suppose," he mumbled. Most people believe the government's low inflation statistics. It's probably much higher. It could be as high as 10% annually.

My lawyer doesn't "get it," doesn't want to "get it." I understand that because almost nobody gets it. Author Simon Black gets it: "Inflation steals from you month after month, year after year. It never stops. Think about it – if they sent gun-toting police to your house demanding 2% of your wealth, there would be rioting in the streets. But if the government and central bank engineer 2% inflation, no one cares. And that's the amazing thing about inflation: governments and academia have managed to convince people that a little bit of inflation is normal."

Baseball salaries are a good way to illustrate inflation. In 1928, Babe Ruth, the greatest baseball player of all time, made $50,000 a year.

In 2018 Los Angeles Angels star Mike Trout made $34 million. The Babe made 1/6 of 1% of Trout's salary. That's .0014. In a way, you could say the money of 1928 has become virtually worthless.

Let's go back 45 years – halfway to 1928. In 1973 Dick Allen of the White Sox was the highest-paid player, after being named the AL's Most Valuable Player the year before. He made $200,000. Do you "get it"? $50,000 – $200,000 – $34,000,000. The rate of depreciation of the dollar is increasing (the bigger it gets, the faster it grows). Somewhere in America today (or in South America), a two year old kid tosses around a rubber ball. In less than 30 years he will earn one billion dollars a year to play baseball.

In 1934 the politicians gained control of the money. The free market had determined that gold and silver were money, but increasingly gold was disparaged. Once the government gained the monopoly on money that allowed politicians to control spending and money creation, the die was cast. It opened the door to ever-expanding social programs, military spending and deficits. Before long, money and credit creation were used to stimulate the economy. Artificially low interest rates (not free market rates) spawned booms that invariably turned into recessions when the money growth slowed or interest rates rose. Today's bubbles are created by excessive money and credit.

Best-selling author Doug Casey explains, "To inflate, a government needs complete control of a country's legal money. This has the widest possible implications, since money is much more than just a medium of exchange. Money is the means by which all other material goods are valued. It represents, in an objective way, the hours of one's life spent in acquiring it. And if enough money allows one to live life as one wishes, it represents freedom as well. It represents all the good things one hopes to have, do, and provide for others. Money is life concentrated.

"As the state becomes more powerful and is expected to provide more resources to selected groups, its demand for funds escalates. Government naturally prefers to avoid imposing more taxes as people become less able (or willing) to pay them. It runs greater budget deficits, choosing to borrow what it needs. As the market becomes less able (or willing) to lend it money, it turns to inflation, selling ever greater amounts of its debt to its central bank, which pays for the debt by printing more money. As the supply of currency rises, it loses value relative to other things, and prices rise. The process is vastly more destructive than taxation, which merely dissipates wealth."

Wall Street doesn't get it, the public doesn't get it, the politicians and bureaucrats most certainly don't get it and, it seems that even the Federal Reserve doesn't get it. They just keep spending, borrowing and printing more money. In 1928, the national debt was $17 billion, in 1968 $347 billion, in 2008 $9 trillion, in 2018 $22 trillion. Government liabilities may now exceed $100 trillion and the astronomical expenses from government social programs are going ballistic. There's no possibility of paying for all this without debasing the currency. Washington claims the inflation rate is low and Wall Street, Main Street and the media buy it hook, line and sinker. Truly they don't "get it."

So far we've been able to avoid the severe inflation that makes our financial affairs completely unmanageable. Certainly we've had inflation. The dollar has lost over 90% of its purchasing power in my lifetime. But we have been able to live with it. Now our bankers, politicians, and brokers wish to encourage inflation. In Washington and Wall Street inflation has gone from being our enemy to our friend and that is crazy. As economist Jörg Hülsmann points out, "Fiat inflation is a juggernaut of social, economic, cultural, and spiritual destruction."

Analyst Alasdair Macleod explains, "The fallacy that the state benefits from inflation ignores our central point: it transfers wealth from the masses. Far from stimulating the economy by persuading the masses to spend rather than save, it gradually grinds them down into poverty. The high standards of living in the advanced economies were acquired over decades by ordinary people working to improve their lives. The accumulation of personal wealth is vital for the enjoyment of improved standards of living. Remove earnings and wealth through currency debasement, and people are simply poorer. And if people are poorer, the finances of the state also become unsustainable.

"This is why regimes that exploit the expansion of money to the maximum, such as Venezuela and Zimbabwe, demonstrably impoverish their people. It takes little intellect to work this out, yet amazingly, neo-Keynesian economists fail to grasp the point. The most appalling example was Joseph Stiglitz, a Nobel prize-winner no less, who ten years ago praised the economic policies of Hugo Chavez. Ten years on, we know the result of Chavez's inflationary follies, which have taken Venezuela and her people into the economic abyss. Despite Stiglitz's execrable errors, he remains an economist respected by those whose biased analyses are simply to wish reality away."

We have been the chief inflationist in the world. We started shipping money around the world to buy things. We exported our inflation for imports. We jacked up price inflation around the world while keeping it under control domestically. Then the rest of the world caught on. They started printing money to pay for their spending just like the U.S. So now we have the entire world inflating. Look at Japan and the European Union covering deficits with the printing press. Now it's not the U.S. alone that will crash and burn, it's the whole world. The late economist Murray Rothbard told us what happens when inflation goes international: "At the end of the road will be a horrendous worldwide hyperinflation, with no way of escaping into sounder or less-inflated currencies."

The inflation of today ruins the plans of retirees and throws many of them into poverty. Inflation also acts as a hidden tax. It impacts the poor, low income workers and those on fixed incomes at exactly the same rate as the rich who can better afford it. This cruel tax, brought to us exclusively by the government, makes poorer those who can least afford it. No person, rich or poor, escapes this terrible depreciation of their money and the subtraction of their purchasing power.

In the history of severe inflations (including the Weimar Republic and two fiat money episodes in 18th-century France) only a few nimble investors and speculators survived and prospered. The vast majority of people lost their shirt. Most of them didn't know or understand what was happening. They didn't "get it." There was much speculation, gambling, debt and leverage, but in the end, all was lost.

Back in 1980 there was an elderly currency analyst by the name of Franz Pick who spoke at monetary conferences. He was fond of saying, "Bonds are certificates of guaranteed confiscation." He may have been premature in 1980, but no longer. Franz Pick got it. He advised investors to own tangible assets that will appreciate at a level that exceeds the rate of inflation. Franz Pick told people, not to wind up on the financial scrap heap with the army of inflation-ravaged investors who didn't "get it." Many retirees and investors are going to get hurt. Be one of the select few who "gets it." Remember that in every big inflation those who listened to government spokesmen lost out. Gold has a history of offsetting inflation. As the dollar goes down, gold tends to go up. You need to own some gold and silver.

CHAPTER XXI
SOCIALISM

"If a thing has to be used as a medium of exchange, public opinion must not believe that the quantity of this thing will increase beyond all bounds. Inflation is a policy that cannot last."
~ Ludwig von Mises

Nothing threatens American freedom like the rise of socialism. The main tenets of socialism are to abolish private property and the market system and turn the ownership of business over to the government. For all intents and purposes socialism and communism are identical. Suddenly socialism has begun to attract adherents in the U.S. Editor Michael Snyder writes, "Americans are increasingly embracing socialism, and this is particularly true for young adults under the age of 30. Four out of every ten Americans now prefer socialism to capitalism, and if current trends continue it is just a matter of time before those that prefer socialism are in the majority."

Author Alex Duke tells us, "Socialism is no longer seen as a threat. Instead, the once-feared ideology is now being celebrated as 'cool.' In certain circles, it carries an automatic claim to virtue. And millennials are being fed the joys of socialism on a daily basis by an increasingly left-leaning media. It was a like-minded media that praised Lenin's implementation of communism as a noble ideal." Its phony promise of equality attracts the welfare class, social warriors, demonstrators and criminals who see a way to distribute other people's wealth to themselves. The possible affiliation of lawbreakers with socialism threatens our civilization. In the last century collectivist governments murdered at least 100 million people. That's never seemed to bother the liberal media outlets like the New York Times. Columnist Marc A. Thiessen writes, "The New York Times has published no fewer than six opinion pieces this year defending communism, including essays praising Lenin as a conservationist, explaining why Stalinism inspired Americans, and arguing that the

Bolsheviks were romantics at heart and that women had better sex under communism."

Ludwig von Mises issued this stark warning to the advocates of socialism: "The worship of the state is the worship of force. There is no more dangerous menace to civilization than a government of incompetent, corrupt, or vile men. The worst evils which mankind ever had to endure were inflicted by bad governments. The state can be and has often been in the course of history the main source of mischief and disaster."

Once these leftists take over a country through elections or revolutions, constitutional protections are quickly eliminated. Those who resist are imprisoned or murdered. That, of course, is the lesson of history. But today's youthful crew of Bernie Sanders followers pay no heed to history. If a belief in socialism spreads to underclass voters and incites the criminals among them, we shall all have reason to fear. No other political idea ever spread so far, so fast or created such misery and failure. However, the New York Times wrote that the collapse of communism in Russia thirty years ago could be the source of socialism's renewal. Granted, we are a long way from electing a socialist government, but so were the Venezuelans and most countries (including the U.S.) are slowly evolving into socialism.

Pope Pius XI wrote in 1931, "Communism teaches and seeks two objectives: unrelenting class warfare and the complete eradication of private ownership. Not secretly or by hidden methods does it do this, but publicly, openly, and by employing any means possible, even the most violent. To achieve these objectives there is nothing it is afraid to do, nothing for which it has respect or reverence. When it comes to power, it is ferocious in its cruelty and inhumanity. The horrible slaughter and destruction through which it has laid waste to vast regions of Eastern Europe and Asia give evidence of this."

It's naïve to believe that any of this has changed or that our nation is impervious to leftist inroads. Watch socialism spread in the months ahead and tell me if I am wrong. Author George Gilder explains, "Socialism in all its forms – from Wall Street subsidy-seekers to bureaucratic profiteers – is in practice a conspiracy of the greedy to exploit the productive. The beneficiaries of the government's transfers of wealth and income smear their betters with the claim of avarice that they themselves deserve. The rich in general have earned their money by contributions to the commonweal that far exceed their incomes, or have inherited their fortunes from forebears who did likewise. What is more, most entrepreneurs continue their work to enrich the world. If you want to see greed in action, listen to leftist college professors denouncing the economic system that provides their freedom, tenure, long vacations, and other expensive privileges."

What the socialists really want is our money. They are driven more by envy than humanitarianism. It doesn't matter to them that socialism makes a country and its inhabitants poorer. No matter how bad the outcome, they will never acknowledge their failure. Once they are in charge, they will kill you to maintain control. All the while the country's prosperity disintegrates. Everyone's life becomes miserable while a few revolutionaries and Marxists live in luxury. The fact that socialists in the U.S. ignore these sorry results in Venezuela, Cuba and Zimbabwe indicates they are more interested in stealing from the wealthy and feathering their own nests than improving society.

In a way it's good that the left is beginning to openly call themselves socialists. For years they got by calling themselves liberals, democrats and progressives, but if you advocate socialist causes you're a socialist. Notice how the U.S. has accepted more and more socialism. The socialist leader Norman Thomas explained, "The American people will never knowingly adopt socialism, but under the name of liberalism, they will adopt every fragment of the socialist program until one day America will be a socialist nation without ever knowing how it happened." Liberalism inevitably morphs into socialism.

The economist Thomas Sowell explains, "The great promise of socialism is something for nothing. It is one of the signs of today's dumbed-down education that so many college students seem to think that the cost of their education should and will be paid by raising taxes on 'the rich.'"

The socialists want free college, free healthcare, free housing, guaranteed jobs, guaranteed incomes, confiscatory taxes, heavy regulation, dictatorial powers and a watered down Constitution. Liberals want the same thing in smaller, more incremental doses. However, the simple fact is that liberal policies eventually get us to full socialism. That's when those who vote for socialism will be rewarded and the wealth of the country confiscated. It's quite simple, if the left wins they will steal everything you have.

Author Joseph Epstein asks, "Does this generation that grows up with a greater sense of entitlement and protection than any other in history really want the revolution Mr. Sanders is selling? Can they have so little sense of the past not to know that the promise of socialism – 'democratic socialism,' the senator would interject here – has ended up in gulags and brutal cultural upheaval?"

Authors Brittany Hunter and Dan Sanchez tell us, "On my college campus, the largest and most active club was the "Revolutionary Student Union," also known as the school's resident Marxists. Even then, I passionately disagreed with socialism. But one thing that struck me was how these students were not only wrong, but seemed deeply unhappy. They always walked into class scowling and were always grousing, not just about the evils of capitalism, but about intractable frustrations and perceived injustices in their personal and academic lives. To these young revolutionaries, every frustration in their lives was someone else's fault. According to their zero-sum Marxist mindset, the prosperity of others came at the expense of their own prospects. So they resented anyone more successful than themselves.

"In spite of all the economic logic and evidence that shows that capitalism enriches and frees the whole of society, while socialism enslaves and impoverishes it, these young socialists would still cling rigidly to their ideology. Why? The socialist frame of mind can be summed up in one word: resentment. As Ludwig von Mises wrote: 'Resentment is at work when one so hates somebody for his more favorable circumstances that one is prepared to bear heavy losses if only the hated one might also come to harm. Many of those who attack capitalism know very well that their situation under any other economic system will be less favorable. Nevertheless, with full knowledge of this fact, they advocate socialism, because they hope that the rich, whom they envy, will also suffer under it.'"

Liberals like to claim they are not socialists. However, they want the government to run things and control the free market system. Unfortunately, there is no half-way between capitalism and socialism. There is only a gradual transition from capitalism to socialism. The mixed economy is a slippery slope to big government and collectivism.

A few years ago I was fortunate enough to visit Rome and stand in the ruins of the Forum. Nothing else quite conveys the grandeur and greatness of Roman civilization. A new book, *The Rise of Rome*, explains the reasons for this success. They're the same reasons the U.S. grew great – "favorable conditions for production and trade." The market economy, with its trade and commerce built Rome. To explain the downfall of the Roman Empire, I rely on the famous historians Will and Ariel Durant. "To support officialdom – the army, the court, public works, and the dole – taxation rose to such heights that men lost incentive to work or earn, and a corrosive contest began between lawyers finding devices to evade taxes and lawyers formulating laws to prevent evasion. Thousands of Romans, to escape the tax gatherer, fled over the frontiers to seek refuge among the barbarians." Doesn't that sound familiar? The same high taxes, big government and excessive regulation that destroyed a once prosperous Roman civilization are in the process of doing the same thing here. Rome began to penalize the successful with confiscatory taxation and reward the unproductive with free bread and entertainment. Eventually under the Emperor Diocletian in 301 A.D., Rome fully embraced socialism. The bureaucrats feathered their own nests and Roman civilization withered and died.

Author Charles Hugh Smith takes a closer look at the Roman decline, "When military and social welfare spending exceed the state's resources to pay the rising costs, the state/empire collapses. The Roman Empire offers an excellent example of this dynamic.

As pressures along the Empire's borders rose, Rome did not have enough tax revenues to fully fund the army. Meanwhile, the costs of free bread and other foodstuffs and public entertainments ('bread and circuses') exhausted the Imperial coffers. Originally intended to alleviate the suffering of the poor, the free bread program had expanded from feeding 40,000 citizens of Rome in 71 B.C. to 320,000 under Augustus – roughly one-third of the entire populace of Rome. Costly entertainments such as bloody gladiator fights that had once been staged on rare public holidays were commonplace by the late Empire, another drain on the state coffers.

"A measure of wheat that cost 6 drachmas in the first century A.D. cost two million drachmas after 344 A.D. How's that for inflation? Today, we face the same crunch: the costs of entitlements are outracing the economy's ability to fund them. Entitlements already consume half the federal budget. To pay for entitlements, federal tax rates will have to double.

"The Romans were not interested in facing the problem. Once the masses became dependent on the free bread, near-riots ensued when the grain shipments were late. Leaders faced with unrest, rising demands and dwindling coffers always debauch their currency as the politically expedient 'solution.' Our own Establishment is readying the free money and printing money to subsidize federal deficits, willfully blind to the eventual destruction of the currency this will inevitably cause."

Ludwig von Mises explains why Rome failed and why we may fail. "Socialism is not in the least what it pretends to be. It is not the pioneer of a better and finer world, but the spoiler of what thousands of years of civilization have created. It does not build; it destroys. For destruction is the essence of it. It produces nothing, it only consumes what the social order based on private ownership in the means of production has created." Mises went on to explain what happens to a civilization that embraces government intervention and socialism. "A society that chooses between capitalism and socialism does not choose between two social systems; it chooses between social cooperation and the disintegration of society. Socialism is not an alternative to capitalism; it is an alternative to any system under which men can live as human beings."

If this frightens you then well it should. We are nearly at the point where the welfare recipients and the subsidized are in control of who wins our elections. That means more government spending and higher taxes until the capitalists and entrepreneurs have been liquidated. Unfortunately, limitless borrowing is impossible and the markets will begin to abuse the dollar. As the value of the currency diminishes in the face of an inflationary holocaust the government will resort to even more socialism. If so, historians will write about the reasons for the decline and fall of America as they do about Rome. Basically Rome disappeared as a viable city. Its population shriveled. With our huge population of subsidized citizens (many of low character) there will be safer places in the world. How do you and your loved ones negotiate the coming events? Paper money is depreciating and one common prescription to offset its demise is to buy gold.

It should be clear to any observer that we are moving away from the things that made us great – limited government, low taxes, free markets, and a rugged individualism that spurned the dole. We cannot survive socialism with any semblance of American greatness. The U.S. with its deficits and runaway government spending is doing a financial high wire act. By embracing more central bank inflation and other socialist schemes we ensure a terrible fall. The Romans never saw their collapse coming. Most Americans are equally clueless. Nothing is so blind as the citizenry of a civilization in decline.

Socialists don't hesitate to slander their opponents. The left in this country likes to link conservatives and libertarians to fascism. They utter warnings about what happened in Nazi Germany happening in America. They also advance the argument that the Nazis were right-wingers and foes of socialism. This, despite the fact the German fascists called themselves National Socialists. Conservative writers have often argued that the Nazis were socialists and had a kinship with the left more than the right.

In doing research for my non-commercial website, neverforget.net, I recently read the book *Hitler – Memoirs of a Confidant*, a book about Otto Wagener. Hitler claimed Wagener was his closest confidant up until 1932. They parted ways because Wagener argued for a peaceful resolution with Russia and the other European countries. Wagener offers many quotes from Adolf Hitler, including this: "It's true that I am a socialist."

Democrats and liberals don't see themselves as socialists, but in many respects they are. It's true that government does not own our industries, but they do extract almost half of what corporations and their employees earn. It's called interventionism. Liberals and progressives are interventionists. It's how they spend the money that makes them socialists. Interventionists and socialists redistribute the money in the same way to the same people.

CHAPTER XXII
EGALITARIAN NONSENSE

"The great merit of gold is precisely that it is scarce; that its quantity is limited by nature; that it is costly to discover, to mine, and to process; and that it cannot be created by political fiat or caprice."

~ Henry Hazlitt

Liberals at the U.S. Securities and Exchange Commission recently approved a rule requiring all companies to disclose the pay gap between the chief executive and the typical worker. This gives a new weapon to groups protesting income inequality. Compliance with this new rule is an added expense for business. Companies will have to disclose the median compensation of all employees and publish a ratio comparing it to the bosses' pay. The late economist Murray Rothbard (1926-1995) explained, "The current veneration of equality is, indeed, a very recent notion in the history of human thought. Among philosophers or prominent thinkers the idea scarcely existed before the mid-eighteenth century; if mentioned, it was only as the object of horror or ridicule."

Attempts to make everybody equal spring from a collectivist mentality. Why is it okay for a football player to make $30 million a year or a singer to make $100 million while a CEO who has run a profitable company with 130,000 employees gets accused of greed? The new rule could be a first step in trying to limit the compensation of business leaders. It would make as much sense to compare what LeBron James makes with the incomes of the fans who pay to watch him. Beyoncé made $115 million in a recent year. How does that compare with the incomes of those who attended her concerts and why isn't the left squawking about that? The contribution to the public well-being by the major corporations who provide our goods and services dwarfs the contribution of actors, athletes and entertainers. This attack on CEO pay by liberals and socialists is an attempt to control all businesses and redistribute profits and incomes.

Economist Hans Sennholz (1922-2007) wrote, "Under the influence of collectivist ideologies, many politicians and journalists are ever eager to strike at successful entrepreneurs who earn much more than they do. It is difficult to ascertain their motives; it can be simple envy which consumes many men, or it can be economic ignorance."

Politicians like Elizabeth Warren want to exert control over corporations to force them to abide by their concept of political correctness and social responsibility. Economist David Stockman made this comment about a new bill she recently introduced: "Senator Elizabeth Warren and her proposed Accountable Capitalism Act is straight out of Atlas Shrugged. She proposes to regulate corporations with gross revenues of $1 billion or more, requiring them to obtain a federal corporate charter as a 'United States corporation.' They would be regulated by a bureaucracy under the Office of United States Corporations. These corporations must be operated to 'create a general public benefit' and must consider how their profit-making activities affect not only their shareholders, but their employees, suppliers, 'community and societal factors,' and the local and global environment. At least 40% of its board of directors must be elected by its workers."

In the world's poorest countries such as Bangladesh, there are virtually no millionaires. In impoverished African nations, wealthy Africans hardly exist. In countries with the most billionaires, living standards are highest and countries with the most new millionaires have the greatest number of people escaping poverty. In other words, when the entrepreneurs of a nation prosper and create wealth, it benefits all the people. Furthermore, when they plow back their earnings to expand their businesses or finance a new business, it grows the wealth of a country even more.

Henry Hazlitt (1894-1993) explained, "No matter whether it is their intention or not, almost anything that the rich can legally do tends to help the poor. The spending of the rich gives employment to the poor. But the saving of the rich, and their investment of these savings in the means of production, gives just as much employment, and in addition makes that employment constantly more productive and more highly paid, while it also constantly increases and cheapens the production of necessities and amenities for the masses." So why do the world's dumbest people want to take away the money that successful people earn? They think it's unfair for someone to make too much. However, people like Jobs and Zuckerman made fortunes because of breakthroughs that changed the world. Those rewards are justified. Big incomes accrue to people who provide superior goods and services. They create jobs and raise living standards, and if they have a lot more money than someone camping under a bridge, isn't that the way it should be?

Inequality also spurs people on. They want more in life so they strive to reach the upper levels of their occupations. Inequality gives all of us examples of what to shoot for. We want what successful people have. Inequality acts as an incentive.

A radical economist like the Frenchman Thomas Piketty, whose book the liberals are swooning over, wants to take away everyone's wealth. Apparently his plan for the money is to give the government more. That sounds more like a plan to exterminate prosperity. France is a nation that's hurt its economy by following the advice of socialists like Piketty.

Most successful business people don't hoard their money. Capitalists give their wealth away to worthwhile causes. Think of Gates in Africa or Sloan and Kettering or the huge gifts from the wealthy to museums, charities, colleges and hospitals. Rich people do good things for society. They are known for their generosity.

The left believes that if one person gets rich it takes away from others. They aren't smart enough to see that if that were true, we could not progress. Capitalism is about giving before receiving and creating new wealth that underlies rising living standards. Impractical leftists who know nothing about economics or business went to implement policies that will make us all poor. They must be stopped. The author Llewellyn Rockwell, Jr. tells us, "We are told how terrible it is that some people should have so much more than others, but rarely if ever are we told how much (if any) extra wealth the egalitarian society would allow the better-off to have." Joseph Sobran (1946-2010) adds, "'Need' now means wanting someone else's money. 'Greed' means wanting to keep your own. 'Compassion' is when a politician arranges the transfer."

Charles Montalembert (1810-1870) wrote, "The reason the state holds up equality as a moral ideal is precisely that it is unattainable. We may forever strive for it, but we can never reach it. 'Equality cannot be imagined outside of tyranny,' said Montalembert. It was, he said, 'nothing but the canonization of envy, [and it] was never anything but a mask which could not become reality without the abolition of all merit and virtue.'

"In the course of working toward equality, the state expands its power at the expense of other forms of human association, including the family itself. The obsession with equality, in short, undermines every indicator of health we might look for in a civilization. It leads to the destruction of standards – scholarly, cultural, and behavioral. It is based on assertion rather than evidence, and it attempts to gain ground not through rational argument but by intimidating opponents into silence. There is nothing honorable or admirable about any aspect of the egalitarian program."

Leftists have called Piketty's *Capital in the Twenty-First Century* "extraordinarily important," and "one of the watershed books in economic thinking." The resident radical at the New York Times, Paul Krugman, calls it "truly superb" and "awesome." Mr. Piketty wants to eliminate high incomes, wealth and what he calls family dynasties. He argues for an 80% tax rate on incomes over $500,000. He advocates an annual wealth tax of 10% on the assets of the rich and a one-time 20% tax on everybody's money. It's not so much that he wants to give it to the poor but to take it away from the affluent. To think that such a horrid prescription could resonate with liberals and cause them such joy tells you what we're up against in America.

Thomas Sowell points out, "What the political left, even in democratic countries, share is the notion that knowledgeable and virtuous people like themselves have both a right and a duty to use the power of government to impose their superior knowledge and virtue on others." In due time the left will have the votes to pull it off. The incredible numbers of people getting subsidies are a powerful voting bloc for the liberals. The poisoning of the minds of minorities and immigrants against what they believe to be social injustice adds more voters to the leftist cause.

Government-sponsored money creation and inflation is the primary cause of income inequality. It makes the wealthy people who own assets that much richer. Inflation shrinks the buying power of wages. The middle class can't keep up because their wage increases are less than the inflation rate. That's the consequence of misleading government statistics and lies about the extent of inflation. If you want to know the real rate of inflation, look backward to prices 10 or 20 years ago.

Mr. Picketty says he believes in free markets and entrepreneurship. However, his formula for eliminating income disparity would lead to poverty. Entrepreneurs would flee the country. Business would wither away and the economy crumble. The lights would go out in America.

Author Michael Lebowitz writes, "Piketty's idea runs perfectly counter to the central precepts laid out in the United States Constitution, the Declaration of Independence, the Pledge of Allegiance, and scores of other important documents that foster the basic tenets of life, liberty and the pursuit of happiness in this country. The challenges capitalism and free markets face are not due to a lack of government imposition of laws and regulation to ensure fairness and justice, they are due to the failure of the United States government to do the primary thing incumbent upon it – defend the rights of liberty as laid out in the founding documents of our country. What Piketty suggests implies a massive expansion of government power in ways that would at a minimum erode and at worst destroy the vitality and dynamism of a capitalistic and free market society. What is most worrisome is that these concepts are not just the ruminations of the latest economic "rock star," they are fully in play in every developed nation and go a long way toward explaining the accumulation of sovereign debt and the deterioration of economic growth in those countries."

In George Gilder's best known book *Wealth and Poverty* (1981) the opening lines read, "The most important event in the recent history of ideas is the demise of the socialist dream." Unfortunately, socialism and collectivism are like Cyborg the character in the movie "Terminator" who can't be killed. No matter how discredited or damaged socialism is or how much evil it's responsible for, it invariably makes a comeback in a slightly new iteration. Editor Marion Smith writes, "Thomas Piketty's *Capital* has provided powerful propagandistic ammunition to neo-Marxists in that battle of ideas, and it is a sad testament to society's short memory of Communism's horrors that *Capital* is the best-selling book in the nation. Its appeal shows that communism is anything but a discredited ideology gasping its last breaths. A generation ago, that was a happy thought. It is now a dangerous illusion."

CHAPTER XXIII
IGNORING RISK

"Gold is not going to fade away and just become another useful metal."

~ Donald J. Hoppe

The other night my wife and I went to a housewarming. It was a large gathering of people, most of whom I didn't know. Always at a loss for much to say at such events, I mentioned a couple of acquaintances the high degree of risk in the world today. One friend thought I meant the risk of getting mugged or having a traffic accident. Another asked if what I meant was risk in financial markets. One acknowledged that his stocks were down but didn't seem to see much risk. My goodness, I thought, how far from the mainstream must I be?

The acid test of intelligence is whether the things you believe in turn out to be true. Thus it's always good to periodically examine one's premises. I regularly immerse myself in the books of the Austrian School economists, Ludwig von Mises, Murray Rothbard, Böhm-Bawerk and Nobel Prize winner Friedrich Hayek. It's made me more certain than ever that we as a nation have drifted so far from rational economic moorings that a monumental financial disorder cannot be avoided.

Today, Austrian economics remains a little known economic school. Contemporary economists totally ignore the Austrian school and question the sanity of anyone who would use this obscure philosophy as the springboard for views that predict financial catastrophe. Nevertheless, Austrian School thinking, however unfashionable, has impressive intellectual credentials. For example, economists from Adam Smith to Karl Marx believed that the value of a thing was determined by the amount of labor that went into making it. Thus Marx could claim that since laborers created the value of things they were due all the profits and that capitalists were cheating them. "Workers of the world unite." From this premise spread the disruptive Marxist philosophy which at times seemed to own the world (especially intellectuals within the United States).

However, in Austria a professor of economics (Böhm-Bawerk, 1851-1941) developed a different explanation of how a thing got value. He knew that ten thousand men could labor to build a pyramid and no one would pay anything for it. But pick up a diamond off an Arkansas hillside and you could sell it for $10,000. Why was gold worth more than silver which was more useful to industry? This was the paradox of value which no economist could resolve.

Böhm-Bawerk knew that you and other consumers are the true arbiters of value. You choose whether an item has value to you. Value is subjective. If you have three wagon loads of grain to last you the winter and you plan to eat one load, use the other for seed and feed the birds with the other, you would naturally price them differently. You would trade the third load for much less than the second. The last (or most recent) sale you make of a bag of grain from your wagon is the present value. It's called marginal utility. The bag with the least marginal utility (value to you) sets the value.

The Austrians solved the value paradox by stating that you don't value the entire world supply of an item, but only a given supply which you can use at that moment. This brilliant analysis became the accepted economic alternative to the value theory of Marxist economists and the core of Austrian economic theory. Economics professor Hans Sennholz stated that the Austrians "thereby managed to place the individual in the center of their analysis and the consumer at the core of the economic order."

Socialists want the state to determine price and value; the Austrians know that only the individual can accomplish this. The buying choices of the individual make the world go round and this free choice is basic to our liberty. The buying choice of the consumer determines profit and loss and the success and failure of businesses products.

In the 1930's, the economic thought of John Maynard Keynes (1883-1946) made an influential mark and relegated the Austrian School to the back of the bus. Among other things, Keynes pushed consumption over savings and government intervention over market solutions. The state manipulated taxes, money supply, government spending and subsidies to foster demand. The politicians loved it and today we are told, "We are all Keynesians." Were he alive today, John Maynard Keynes would cringe at our low savings, debt monetization and interest rate meddling. He would refuse to take any blame for such extremes.

Austrian economics bases its views on the actions of individuals. These actions can't be codified because of the unpredictable responses people will give to each circumstance. You prefer chewing gum while I like breath mints. You buy a pack at a time, I go to Sam's and load up. Modern economics tends to treat us like so many units, with algebraic certainty. Economic outcomes cannot be determined by laws similar to physics. Austrian economics does not lend itself to mathematics. Professor Mises dismissed mathematical analysis as unworkable. Economics is a branch of philosophy and not an exercise of math. Yet, the most influential mathematical economist in the United States today does not recognize Austrian economics because it does not lend itself to mathematics.

Today we inflate at will. Fiat money created out of thin air, runaway government borrowing, huge government financial guarantees, staggering levels of leverage in securities markets, consumer credit excesses, negative savings rates and monstrous trade and budget deficits have created a financial house of cards. Mises warned that the employment of these policies leads to economic disaster and makes a collapse inevitable. Mises is the economist whose views you should listen to, not the Marxists and socialists of academia, not the Wall Street and Washington Keynesians who manipulate interest rates and money supply.

The late economist and professor Hans Sennholz (1922-2007) was a student of Ludwig von Mises. He wrote, "If we cannot return to fiscal integrity because the public prefers profusion and prodigality over balanced budgets, we cannot escape paying the price, which is ever lower incomes and standards of living for all. The pains of economic stagnation and decline which are plaguing us today are likely to intensify and multiply in the coming years. The social and racial conflict, which springs from the redistribution ideology, may deepen as economic output is shrinking and transfer 'entitlements' cause budget deficits to soar. The U.S. dollar, which has become a mere corollary of government finance, is unlikely to survive the soaring deficits."

He explained how government deficits expand. "When the public demand for government services and benefits grows beyond the ability of business and wealthy taxpayers to pay, budgetary deficits become unavoidable. After all, the popularity of redistribution by political force tends to grow with every dollar of 'free' service rendered. The clamor finally becomes so intense that, in order to be heard, every new call is presented as an 'emergency' that must be met immediately before all others. Redistributive government then rushes from one emergency to another, trying to meet the most noise and politically potent demands."

Mr. Sennholz explained the nasty consequences of America's financial bubbles. "Many failed to recognize the gradual development of financial bubbles especially in equity markets and real estate. Bubbles, which ultimately must deflate and come to naught, are difficult to spot because they closely resemble real economic expansion. They look like genuine capital formation which causes interest rates to decline, profits to rise, and asset prices to advance. Actually, they are visible symptoms of maladjustments caused by wanton money and credit creation and false interest rates. They enjoy the loud support and confirmation by the monetary authorities blowing the bubbles and by politicians who love the booms.

"While true economic expansion builds on genuine saving and capital formation, a financial bubble springs from deliberate money and credit creation which falsifies interest rates and goods prices, misleads businessmen and consumers, wastes productive capital, and benefits a few speculators at the expense of multitudes of investors."

In my book, *The Start-up Entrepreneur*, I quoted F. W. Woolworth, who claimed that Dutch businessmen of Puritan stock taught him how to flourish in business without borrowing money. Contrast the go-go world of today's easy money with the way things once were when gold was money. "They ran their stores on the same policy for more than half a century; they did not progress, except as a tree progresses in size. They grew wealthy slowly, but surely. They never went into debt; they always paid for what they bought, and paid with cash. They bought at the lowest price, and they bought not a cent's worth more than they actually needed. When they put money in the bank – salted it away – it was put away to stay. There were no liens on anything they owned. These Dutch farmers taught me to manage my own business and never to let my business manage me."

CHAPTER XXIV
WITHOUT MERIT

"Never have the world's moneys been so long cut off from their metallic roots."
~ Murray M. Rothbard

Forty-five years ago, I left a comfortable family business and went to Miami to start a drinking water company. This endeavor was a huge personal struggle, full of financial peril, rejection and anxiety. I devoted a chapter to this ordeal in my book, *The Start-up Entrepreneur.* Fortunately, after more than a year of work and strain a wealthy family made me an offer I couldn't refuse and I sold out to them. For a few months after that I was in the chips.

I returned to Minnesota and with a partner started Investment Rarities. In two years (1975) our money was gone and we were on the ropes. One crisis led to another. At a critical moment my partner buckled. He proclaimed our venture was defunct and tried to leave with one of our few remaining assets. We had a falling out. I bought his stock for very little. He left me with a load of debt and unpaid bills.

At the moment we stared failure in the face he quit while I persisted. He had no faith in our future while I was sure we would ultimately succeed. Why? I had an enormous advantage over him. I had previously suffered through the despair and pain of near failure in my water business. This had strengthened me. My partner lacked persistence because he had no prior experience with struggle. In his previous enterprise he had made a lot of money without paying much of a price. Things had been easier for him.

The founder of U.S. Steel, Andrew Carnegie, strived for success in business so that he "should never again be called upon to endure such nights and days of racking anxiety." I have suffered through these severe business droughts and cyclical downturns over the past four decades and one thing stands out. The struggles of life teach the truly valuable lessons. We learn little from good times and virtually nothing from success. Emerson said it best. "When man [or woman]…is pushed, tormented, defeated, he has a chance to learn something; he has been put on his wits, on his manhood, he has gained facts, learns his ignorance, is cured of the insanity of conceit; has got moderation and real skill."

Now suppose that at the inception of my Miami water business there was a government program for young men that awarded me a large contract. My life would have been so much easier. I would have been an immediate success. At first glance this would have helped me enormously, but in reality it would have crippled me. I would have missed the lessons and struggles that had made me resourceful. Every bout of pain in life makes the next round more likely to be endured.

The government has programs and requirements that give money, or business contracts to women and minorities. These preferences supposedly help the recipient. But they do not. They simply relieve these people from learning the necessary lessons required to climb to the top and succeed on merit.

Those who oppose these government preferences are thought to be mean-spirited or reactionary. The media brands them as chauvinists or racists. In reality, most business owners or managers want a level playing field and would like to see minorities and women reach the upper levels of achievement. Most men in business want all people to experience success and are not in the least threatened by this prospect. But those of us who have struggled time and again know that this can never be accomplished with shortcuts. The government's subsidy programs will ruin the chances of minorities and women to take their place on the pinnacles of success. If you accept business contracts or money you didn't earn to speed your success, you undermine your long-term prospects and incur the dead opposite of what the government strives to accomplish.

If you get a job or promotion because of your race or gender, it is no different than a subsidy. You get something that you didn't earn, something for nothing. You are weaker for it than if you climbed the ladder by yourself. It may seem like a helping hand, but if it deprives you of skill and inner strength it is a push backwards. Nothing good ever comes from getting something you didn't earn.

Now the government and the media encourages those who get entitlements to see themselves as victims. This is just one more horribly negative outcome of subsidies. Once trapped in the belief that you are a victim, you surrender your birthright to compete for the prizes of life. In the mind of the victims and their sponsors, everything controversial that happens in the country becomes just another plot to keep them from succeeding. Such perceptions can easily become reality.

It's not just the underclass that suffers from something-for-nothing. A corollary exists with the children of wealthy people who shield their offspring from economic struggle. If you are affluent and want to harm your children, give them all the money they will ever need. If you leave them your fortune before they've made their own way, they will be weaker for it. Rich or poor, insulate youngsters from life's struggles and you will fashion people who cannot stand on their own, cannot build, accomplish or create.

The left recently started promoting the idea of a Universal Basic Income. Editor Michael Pento writes, "The ultra-liberal co-founder of Facebook, Chris Hughes, is pushing for a guaranteed income of $500 a month for every working adult who makes less than $50,000, paid for by raising taxes on people who make over $250k or more. And by working he doesn't necessarily mean having a paying job – working can be defined as just having a dependent child. Of course, UBI also provides an ever-growing voting class that will become dependent on the government for everything. Perhaps this is more the real goal."

Investor's Business Daily wrote, "In recent weeks, the idea of a 'universal basic income' has shown surprising popularity. For the left, the case for a guaranteed income, is that not everyone can compete in today's high-tech, advanced economy. The real problem is that when you hand a person a check they have less incentive to work. Period. It is an ironclad rule of economics: What you subsidize, you incentivize. Subsidize non-work through a guaranteed income, and don't be surprised when lots of people stop working. And someone else will pay for it. Is that the kind of society we seek? The truth is, a guaranteed income is a very bad idea. It's utopian, and anti-work. America is based on work, is defined by it. At this point in our history, shouldn't we be looking for ways to encourage work, not discourage it?

Author George Gilder explains the weakness of this liberal bromide: "If everyone gets supported without any kind of growing up and facing the challenges of life, then our capitalist culture would collapse." Michael Pento explains further, "Universal Basic Income (UBI) makes payments to people for doing absolutely nothing. UBI is a handout. As bizarre as this may sound, it is rapidly gaining worldwide traction. Doling out free money stifles the incentive for workers to adapt. We see these effects when there are long extensions in benefits for unemployment, like the Great Recession. While unemployment insurance is useful as a short-term stopgap between jobs, continuous extensions of unemployment leads to complacency. During the Great Recession, many transitioned off unemployment onto long-term disability, putting a drain on the current social safety net. Comprehensive welfare programs such as Universal Basic Income, soon lead to a perpetual condition of economic stagnation, higher interest rates, currency depreciation, rising debt-to-GDP ratios, onerous tax rates and rapid inflation."

CHAPTER XXV
CONSEQUENCES

"The gold standard sooner or later will return with the force and inevitability of natural law, for it is the money of freedom and honesty."

~ Hans F. Sennholz

I had a few hours to kill on a recent Sunday before a flock of grandkids showed up to open Christmas presents. Since I was caught up on my reading I clicked on the TV and channel surfed until I came across the 1965 movie, Dr. Zhivago, which was just starting. The part I remembered and wanted to see again came about halfway through the movie. The doctor, played by Omar Sharif, had returned to Moscow after two years at the front in World War I. The Bolsheviks were now firmly entrenched, running the country.

Zhivago had married into a wealthy family before the war and when he returned to their large and once lovely household he was in for a shock. A couple of dozen shabbily dressed party members had taken over the house. He and his family were relegated to one bedroom. Any complaints about their misfortune would be cause for arrest. They acquiesced to this theft of their property out of fear.

Frankly, the difference between the Russian Bolsheviks and today's leftists in American isn't that great. They differ only by a matter of degree. The Communists in Russia got everything you owned. So far the liberals have only been successful in getting almost half of what you earn, plus a healthy slice of what you own when you die. Philosophically, the liberals, the Marxists and the socialists are blood brothers. They all wish to address social injustice, raise taxes, put the government in control of the economy and redistribute the wealth of the nation through subsidies. Their heightened sense of social sympathy makes them antagonistic to the accomplishments of capitalism. Their outrage over the inequality of incomes overrides any concern for the dire economic consequences of their policies.

What the liberals stand for has always failed when put into practice. It is failing now before our eyes. It will always fail. These leftist schemes promise national ruin. That the historical failure of collectivism is not properly acknowledged by the left speaks of their myopic stubbornness.

Once you commit the first dollar to a government social program it's the beginning of the end. The number of these programs never stops expanding. At first there was one, now there are hundreds. Furthermore, the existing programs never stop growing and costs rise relentlessly. You have a three-headed monster; new programs, growth of existing programs and runaway costs of all programs. When the government can't pay for them they borrow or print new money to keep them funded. This debases our currency, acts as a hidden tax and spreads a contagion of ills associated with inflation. It's how nations go bankrupt.

My wife and I disagreed recently about subsidized day care. Someone we know was attempting to get this assistance. It would free her fiancé up from babysitting and he could get a job. My wife thought that this was a worthwhile government program. I claimed that this was not a proper function of government. What would the founding fathers think of a government that, among other things, was collecting taxes to dispense to people for someone to take care of their kids? My wife's eyes glazed over.

No question, day care is necessary and the market system makes it widely available. If someone can't afford it, then private charities should be available to help them. However, the government has assumed the role of charities and private institutions. Consequently, there is no need for a private charitable response. It's just another responsibility that has been turned over to the state.

Private charity is more discerning about who is deserving and who isn't. It's not wasteful. It's not permanent and it generally makes people begin to rely on themselves. Private charity can apply "tough love" but government never can. While government charity gives the most to those who refuse to help themselves, private charity gives less. Private charity improves society and the human condition.

Government subsidies make it worse.

Now, if someone argues against this government system, they can easily be portrayed as a nut. Who would argue against poor people or working moms having day care for their children? Who would suggest that we take this assistance away? In other words, once this government program is embedded, it's impossible to ever end it. Since it would harm people to terminate government subsidized day care, it will never happen. There is no charitable alternative. At the time it was first proposed, the best case could be made against it. Now it's too late. Like all government social programs, it cannot be turned back or ended, it can only be expanded.

Someday, this program will end along with most other social schemes, including subsidized housing, Medicare, and food stamps. That's because their costs cannot be controlled. When taken in total, they can bankrupt the nation. As their costs rise, taxes must also rise, thus hurting business reducing the amount of taxes collected. Eventually the government will be unable to fund its social programs. This will not be a happy time for anybody.

Too sad to contemplate is the fate of a quarter of our population who are on the dole. If the dollar doesn't buy much what happens to them? How will they survive? What kind of threat do they represent to the rest of us? No country has ever subsidized so many and no country has ever suffered hyperinflation because of it. This is a mess of our own making and the outcome will fill the pages of history. Get ready for national convulsions.

That's not the worst of it. Government social programs don't work. None of them accomplish what they set out to do. In fact, they make matters worse. We've spent hundreds of billions to eradicate poverty. Yet the economic and social condition of welfare recipients is worse than when these programs started. Despite public housing, rent subsidies, food stamps, welfare payments and more, the long-term recipients of entitlements have essentially become a hoard of drug addicts and alcoholics.

Worst of all, the attitudes of the underclass and their sympathizers have turned into a frightful animosity towards the prevailing culture. The more money they get the louder their accusations of racism, inequality and injustice. The more they are subsidized, the more they express hatred for America, curse capitalism and support a radical agenda. They make up false charges to justify their shakedown of America. Their leadership gains money and power while encouraging a belief in victimhood.

Whatever you subsidize, you get more of. That's why the numbers of the unproductive are overtaking the producers. When that day ultimately comes we are all Doctor Zhivagos, sharing our property through government edicts. It's quite possible America will go broke first and the social welfare edifice will be dismantled. On the other hand we could all be collectivized. Whatever the outcome, one thing stands as an historical certainty. We will either do away with socialism or socialism will do away with us.

The U.S. reminds me of a person who suddenly makes a lot of money, gets bigheaded and blows their fortune on high living. Usually they wind up suffering through financial reversals and a lengthy period of personal austerity. They are humbled by these struggles. Often we hear that these painful experiences changed them for the better. Perhaps the same rules apply to countries. A country that experiences austerity and bankruptcy may emerge from this humiliating period with its people more self-sufficient and its industries more productive. In that sense a national comeuppance, with all its agonies may be a good thing. Eventually the people come to understand there is no free lunch. They work more and play less. Behavior and character improve. Here in the U.S. we have reached a level of excess that betrays our legacy and ensures our collapse. Public and private debt, runaway government spending and fiat money have hit the wall. We can't go back and going forward invites retribution. A national humbling and painful austerity are inevitable. The ferocity of the crisis will be correlated to the degree of excess, so it will be large and painful.

I suspect we are going to have runaway inflation. Hyperinflation doesn't last long. Wealth gets reshuffled and a lot of people lose their money. People with tangible assets can survive and even do well. Foreign currencies, hard assets and money with gold backing replace the dying currency. That's the way it went in Weimar Germany until they issued a new currency. It was painful but not terminal for those who owned tangibles.

Have you ever seen film clips of a rocket ship leaving earth? At first you see nothing but flat surface, then you begin to see the earth's curvature. Soon the earth becomes a large ball and then begins to shrink to the size of an orange. Before long, the earth is the size of a dime. That's what happens to your money after you retire. After twenty years of retirement your savings, bonds and annuities, that were once so comforting, have shrunk in purchasing power like the diminishing earth.

Let's face it, the government's inflation figures aren't trustworthy. Inflation across the board is at least 5% year over year. Furthermore, runaway federal spending promises more inflating as government creates new money to pay for its wayward social schemes. Over a lifetime the dollar has lost 98% of its value and the pace of decline seems to be quickening. The earth becomes the size of a pea and then a BB.

People that don't have current income (no matter how much money they have) tend to cut back and curtail their lifestyle. They worry to some degree about money. The longer you live, the greater the likelihood that government sponsored inflation will eat away much of your savings. One thing is for sure, if you take it on the chin and do nothing but watch your savings shrink, you can wind up with nothing.

At some point it will dawn on the populace that prices are going to keep rising because the central bank and the Treasury are going to persist in creating new money. More and more people will decide to spend the money rather than hold it because they know they can get goods cheaper today than they can tomorrow. Suddenly there's a rush to buy things.

We are often asked what would a person use for purchases during and after a runaway inflation. As one client pointed out, you wouldn't take a one-ounce gold coin to purchase a gallon of ice cream at a convenience store. I can only speculate on the answer based on the Weimar Republic inflation in Germany in 1921. The government would certainly be on top of this so there would only be a brief period with a worthless currency that bought nothing. Up to that point, prices would be jumping daily. Gas would go to $5 a gallon one week and $10 the next. The following week gas would be $50 a gallon and then $100 and in the third week, $500 a gallon. You would still be using dollars for purchases during this period of rising prices. Wages would be trying to keep up. This is when gold, silver, diamonds and other tangibles would save you just as they saved people in the German inflation. These tangible assets would appreciate at close to the inflation rate, providing you with the necessary purchasing power to survive. You would convert a gold coin into dollars and immediately spend it to avoid the ongoing and immediate depreciation. For example if you wanted to buy two weeks of groceries for your family you would sell the gold coin for $100,000 and immediately buy the two weeks of groceries you needed for the same $100,000. Periods like this don't last long because when people lose faith in the currency's ability to hold value they begin to spend it as fast as they can to buy real goods.

Annuities, savings, money markets and bonds will have quite suddenly lost all value. Along with the dollar they are worthless. The government's Social Security checks and other payments effectively bounce. They buy nothing. Washington's politicians and the Treasury announce a new currency. However, it's too late for the millions of savers and investors who relied on government to fix the economy. They lost everything.

This destructive period would likely be over in a few weeks. Perhaps foreign currencies would come into use and silver coins would gain immediate recognition at the cash register. Something takes the place of a failed currency almost immediately. Remember how cigarettes were the means of exchange in post-war Germany. Furthermore, the government would be frantically engaged in issuing a new currency to replace the depreciated dollar. They did that after the Weimar inflation and things began to settle down fairly soon. It's only that brief period when the currency fails completely that you have to find a way to survive comfortably. Most tangible assets would maintain their value with gold and silver among the best of these because of their liquidity and portability.

Most people scorn the possibility of runaway inflation. The mainstream media looks at such concerns as nutty. However, enough people ask about what to use for money in a hyperinflation that we need to have an answer. Is it possible that the dollar could suffer such a massive depreciation? According to the Austrian School of economics it's probable.

You may think all of this sounds far fetched. From my perspective I think it's inevitable. Years ago much smarter economists than me wrote about the certainty of such an event. We are going to face national bankruptcy. We brought it on ourselves by embracing ruinous policies. We let liberalism run wild. The sorry outcome is now inevitable. Hope for the best but prepare for the worst.

CHAPTER XXVI
LIBERAL BIAS

"I see a great future for gold and silver coins as the currency people may increasingly turn to when paper currencies begin to disintegrate."
~ Murray M. Rothbard

In 1984 my first book was published and I went to New York to do some TV shows that my public relations firm had arranged. I also met with the executive editor of a well-known national magazine. My wife and I joined her and an assistant at a fashionable New York eatery. Over lunch I was to give her a rundown on why my book would appeal to readers of her magazine. We never got that far.

Almost immediately she began to talk about Nicaragua and the revolutionary Sandinistas who had recently overthrown the government there. She championed their cause to me and heaped praise on Danny Ortega, their Marxist leader. Then she began to inquire about my views on the matter. I was in an awkward spot. I despised these revolutionary leftists, but if I mentioned my true sentiments, the book review was going out the window. I professed to be not paying much attention to what was happening in Central America. Immediately her assistant sized me up as one of those Midwest hicks who needed a lesson in liberalism. Clearly courting the favor of her superior, she gave me a brief history lesson on Nicaragua and lectured my wife and I on why we should sympathize with the revolutionaries.

We could easily have had an argument, but I held my tongue. Nevertheless, they didn't write a single paragraph about my book. I always felt that it was because I didn't show enough enthusiasm over their cherished Sandinistas. I did learn, however, how passionate about left-wing causes New York magazine publishers could be, and I saw how assistant editors who shared this view were far more likely to get promoted than others. To this day I know in my heart that in music, the arts, book reviews and entertainment, those who get featured in the press and other media share liberal political views with those who dispense the publicity. It explains why the modern art movement of the twentieth century (centered in New York) mostly emanated from artists who are radicals, socialists and Marxists. These artists whose paintings sell for millions today were denizens of the far left. That might explain why modern art fails to register with most Americans. They don't like it.

It's no wonder. An article about the highly important opening of the renovated Museum of Modern Art in New York said this: "Chris Ofili, who generated a firestorm of controversy at the Brooklyn Museum of Art with his painting of a dung-dusted Madonna, is also on view with another portrait, this one *sans* Mary, but still with the dung, coated with glitter so it catches the light." How nice.

Sadly, it may not be possible to make it big in the arts today unless you're a darling of the left-wing New York media. But more people are catching on. Their manipulation of the news has become transparent. Instead of just listening to the news, many of us now monitor it for liberal bias. They never disappoint, it's always there and, no matter how subtle their spin, we can see through it.

Yes, these are the same people who loved Danny Ortega in Nicaragua. Before that it was Castro, the "agrarian reformer," who impressed the liberals. Years ago conservatives warned of falling dominoes in Southeast Asia and the left heaped scorn on that view. Eventually countries did fall like dominoes and the communists butchered two million innocents in Cambodia. Lately it's been hostility toward Israel. Whatever it is, you can be sure that it's wrong. Editor Bob Tyrell writes, "For some reason, our media are fascinated by stories that appear to harm American national interests."

How did our country drift so far towards big government and socialism? It was never this way. Throughout my lifetime we kept moving leftward embracing one government program after another. In my family we listened to the national news every night at 5:30 P.M. Edward R. Murrow, Walter Kronkite, Huntley and Brinkley fed us a steady diet promoting big government and undermining capitalism. The major networks were all left-leaning and the newspaper and magazines were even more liberal. Big city dailies like the New York Times and Washington Post published the progressive agenda and magazines like Time and Newsweek became rabid advocates of big government. Unfortunately, none have ever confronted the massive failures they helped engineer.

Recently Warren Buffet has been getting a lot of ink. Why? He came out for raising taxes. That's the way it works. Liberals have totally infiltrated the publishing business. Recently, my wife bought tickets to hear an author talk about his novel that was set in Germany in the years after the war. He was formerly an editor at a New York publishing house. His talk was interesting. Prior to World War II a number of German socialists and communists fled Germany for California. After the war, a handful of them, including the playwright Bertolt Brecht, returned to East Germany which was then a Russian satellite. The novel takes place in this era. I found his talk to be more interesting than the novel.

After the program, several in the audience lined up to buy an autographed copy of the book and have a brief conversation with the author. Since I've always wondered how widespread German guilt was for the atrocities of the Second World War, I asked him if the Germans feel guilt. "Heavens no," he replied, "They don't feel any collective guilt." Then he said, "Look what we've done."

It didn't really register with me until later. What he apparently meant was that the U.S. was guilty of crimes against humanity that equaled those of Nazi Germany. I was dumbfounded, but realized this was a popular view among radicals and socialists. This extremely opinionated man was a New York City liberal convinced of his intellectual superiority. New Yorkers believe they are culturally superior to begin with, but when you couple that with liberal intolerance they are downright unbearable. Yes, New York liberals are a pain in the neck, many are radicals and some are so screwed up they think America has acted worse than Nazi Germany.

Liberals like this have no respect for the values of most Americans. Author Dinesh D'Souza writes, "Psychologist Nicholas Humphrey argued in a recent lecture that secular teachers and professors should work to free children from the damaging influence of their parents' religious instruction. 'Parents, correspondingly, have no God-given license to enculturate their children in whatever ways they personally choose: no right to limit the horizons of their children's knowledge, to bring them up in an atmosphere of dogma and superstition, or to insist they follow the straight and narrow paths of their own faith.'

"Philosopher Richard Rorty argued that secular professors in the universities ought 'to arrange things so that students who enter as bigoted, homophobic religious fundamentalists will leave college with views more like our own.' Rorty noted that students are fortunate to find themselves 'under the benevolent Herrschaft [dominion] of people like me, and to have escaped the grip of their frightening, vicious, dangerous parents.' Indeed, parents who send their children to college should recognize that as professors 'we are going to go right on trying to discredit you in the eyes of your children, trying to strip your fundamentalist religious community of dignity, trying to make your views seem silly rather than discussible."

If it's not one thing it's another with liberals. In addition to an anti-religious bias, they've been cozying up to radical Islam, slandering the rich, knocking Israel, promoting an extreme environmental agenda, finding racism everywhere, despising capitalism, hating white males, espousing socialism and lobbying for open borders. The writer Joe Sobran put it best. "Liberalism's fatal flaw…is that it has no permanent norms, only a succession of enthusiasms espoused by minor prophets. Each of these seems like a hot new idea to liberals, but soon goes to irksome and destructive extremes."

Another bill of goods the media has tried to sell us concerns the supposedly superior health care available in communist Cuba. How often have we heard about the great health care in Cuba? Author Mona Charen writes, "The myth of Cuba's wonderful, free, universal health care system will not die. President Obama lauded it. Michael Moore beatified it. Bernie Sanders cited it to shame the United States by comparison! What can you say to people with such a profound need to believe? There are actually three health services in Cuba. There is one for tourists, featuring state-of-the-art equipment. There is a second for high-ranking Communists, the military, approved artists and so forth. This, too, is a good system. And then there is the squalid, dirty, understaffed, massively under-equipped medical system that ordinary Cubans (the vast majority) must endure. In the third system, overworked doctors reuse latex gloves, antibiotics are scarce, and patients must 'bring their own bed sheets, soap, towels, food, light bulbs – even toilet paper.' A 2014 report from the Institute for War and Peace Reporting found that in Cuban hospitals 'the floors are stained and surgeries and wards are not disinfected. Doors do not have locks and their frames are coming off. Some bathrooms have no toilets or sinks, and the water supply is erratic. Bat droppings, cockroaches, mosquitoes and mice are all in evidence.' And yet, even such an august publication as The Atlantic published a piece after Castro's death titled 'How Cubans Live as Long as Americans at a Tenth of the Cost.'"

CHAPTER XXVII
KEEPING WHAT YOU HAVE

"Gold is as steady as a rock, a standard bearer by which all currencies can be accurately measured."
~ Mark Skousen

The average investor thinks more about making money than about keeping it. People focus on gains or income but pay little attention to the threat of losing in a major way. Virtually no one prepares against the risk of great loss. They belittle the idea of a crash or panic that bankrupts the institutions and wipes them out personally. We have been rolling along for seven or more years without a major financial setback or bear market and most people have forgotten the past.

Analyst John Hussman warns, "Across centuries of history, speculative financial bubbles have repeatedly emerged. The speculative behavior of the crowd results in rising prices that both impress and reward speculators, and in turn encourage even greater speculation. The more impressed the crowd becomes with the result of its own behavior, the more that behavior persists, and the more unstable the system becomes, until finally the flapping wings of a butterfly become sufficient to provoke a collapse. Across history, the evaporation of paper wealth following periods of speculation has repeatedly taught a lesson that is never retained for long. Unfortunately, the lesson has to be relearned again and again because of what J.K. Galbraith referred to as 'the extreme brevity of the financial memory.' Speculation is dangerous because it encourages the belief that just because prices are elevated, they must somehow actually belong there."

If you have ever started a business and tried to make a profit, you know how tough it is to make money. It can take years of work and struggle to get into the black. Recently, it's been easier to make money investing in stocks. In the past you needed patience coupled with sound investment principles to make money in stocks. Now stock gains come quickly and most investors seem to profit. However, the economist Martin Feldstein offers this warning: "An excessively easy monetary policy has led to overvalued equities and a precarious financial situation."

Most wealthy men and women turn their finances over to professional money managers. Lately they've been turning to hedge funds. These managers also tend to run in packs. They pretty much follow the investment logic of Warren Buffet who pointed out that twice in his career his stock portfolio fell by half. He only had to have patience and in time it recovered and grew from there. All these folks buy into the theory that everything will be fine and recoveries are inevitable. None of them understand that we face an unfolding crisis that can vaporize much of their wealth. What's happened in the past may not happen again.

Throughout history, there have been regular intervals when credit collapses, panics, hyper-inflations and depressions ruined countries and currencies and turned the rich into paupers. Nobody worries about a big crash or panic. The widespread belief that the government won't let anything bad happen reinforces the view that they are immune to destructive losses and this time it's different. Consequently, almost no one takes any measure at all to protect themselves against the financial plagues that have regularly afflicted mankind. Mutual fund pioneer Sir John Templeton (1912-2008) warns us, "The four most dangerous words in investing are 'This time is different.'"

Not only are many individuals totally invested in stocks and mutual funds, they have their entire retirement plan committed to equities. Some add leverage to the mix and borrow additional money for stocks. Others run down cash balances and savings to buy stocks. A dip in stock prices fosters additional buying rather than serious concern about further declines. Virtually all of today's investors are on the offensive. People apply the least shrewd thinking to their retirement money. Here's the mindset: Our retirement plan is a long-term investment and we will leave it in stocks through rain or shine and it will always trend higher in the long run. Eventually any loss will be made up. That thinking may make more sense at the end of a bear market but not when the bull has broken all the records. People who believe the Wall Street propaganda about a permanent boom will be hurt by a bear market. The bear can bring a financial disaster and a kind of fear that changes the way people behave and think for years to come.

Everyone in the market makes the assumption that they can get out before a big downward slide. In other words, they will be able to see trouble before other investors and thus make their exit. Past market reversals generally follow a pattern of steep repetitive drops wiping out as much as half the bull market gains within a few weeks. The bear doesn't ring a warning bell. The way people have deluded themselves about a perpetual bull market means that many will decide to weather the decline. These folks will keep on believing that it will bounce back. They will hold till late in a decline and thereby sacrifice years of gains. In the worst bear market drops, it's entirely possible that you can't get out at anywhere near the quoted price. With enough sellers and a panic atmosphere, bids vanish and prices go through the floor. Sell orders get triggered at much lower prices. Mutual fund liquidations may be held up for days. At times, in severe shakeouts you can't get out at all. The idea that the stock market possesses unparalleled liquidity is a myth.

Eighty-nine years ago the country struggled in a depression that lasted eight years. Severe stock market losses wiped out the wealth of investors and illustrated that it's entirely possible to lose everything in a market crash. Whenever such an event begins, fear turns into panic, losses jump quickly and values evaporate. Today's investors will turn nasty should the bear strike in earnest. John Hussman warns us, "This whole speculative mania will end tragically. How did we not learn this from 2000-2002, or 2007-2009, or the collapse of every other mania in history?"

As it did in 1929, when it started a depression, another great stock crash can lead to a steep plunge in business activity. Confidence fades fast in a financial crisis. Consumer spending slows and savings rise. With the massive amount of credit card debt, consumer loans and extremes of leverage throughout the financial system a stiff recession can turn nasty. That's when people lose their jobs, can't pay their bills, have their cars repossessed and lose their homes. Analyst Larry Parks tells us, "With the monetary system we have now, the careful saving of a lifetime can be wiped out in an eye-blink." It appears to be a time when defensive measures make sense. Author William Alexander writes, "The U.S. economy is like a guy that jumped out of a plane with no parachute and because he hasn't hit the ground yet, he thinks he's ok."

It's pure speculation on my part, but having watched carefully the market corrections of the past few years, it seemed that each time a downturn threatened to get out of hand, a powerful surge of buying would appear. Could this be a buying pool of banks or brokerage firms financed in some way by the monetary authorities? This would account for the unprecedented bull market because normal corrections were never allowed to run their course. If it is it true, it would set the stage for an even greater market collapse.

Years ago Chairman Alan Greenspan's said in a speech he gave in Belgium, "We have the responsibility to prevent major financial market disruptions through development and enforcement of prudent regulatory standards and, if necessary, in rare circumstances through direct intervention in market events." Say what? Regulators have the responsibility of direct intervention in markets? This certainly represents a dramatic broadening of the role of the Central Bank. We need more clarification on this point. However, if the aim is to support the dollar, bolster the stock market, hold up the bond market, keep the economy humming, and fight inflation, even the most powerful interventionists can bite off more than they can chew and wind up failing at all of these.

Even government securities can turn sour if the credit-worthiness of government comes into question. Throughout history those governments that spent wantonly and borrowed recklessly often defaulted. The citizens of these countries never got advance notice. They were wiped out. In our modern era when gold has no role as money and nothing can put a brake on monetary expansion the Central Bank can monetize any amount of debt. So rather than default, the government can inflate the debt away. In either case the bondholder gets killed. Analyst Tom Chatham writes, "When a national currency collapses, the government goes into survival mode and does what is necessary to ensure its continued existence. Should the government confiscate resources following a collapse, you will need to be two steps ahead of them and the general population in order to get through the events in one piece."

Analyst Alasdair Macleod argues, "Far from deflation, the Fed's only response to the next credit crisis will be to take measures that will lead to the final destruction of the dollar. Other central banks are set to follow. Deflationists don't have a leg to stand on."

People have the mistaken belief that good times can't change. Few have the historical perspective to understand just how much suffering past economic failures have caused. They don't appreciate how good this country has had it or what a remarkably luxurious life they have. Most people who lived in prior times suffered in conditions we would consider harsh and cruel. The periodic loss of what little they had was the nature of things.

When you have high levels of money and credit creation funneling into stocks, along with rampant leverage, record margin debt, inflated stock values, and swollen historical ratios, you have far greater potential for a monumental bust. We're not talking about a simple correction, we're talking about a crash. Blood does not run in the streets after a period of prudent investment and modest speculation. But it does occur following excesses similar to those present in today's market. Nevertheless, the public remains impervious to just how lethal things can get. History shows us that booms turn to busts. The term "bear market" defines what used to be a frequent market phenomenon.

Tom Chatham writes, "Numerous economists and investors are warning of another great financial crisis to come but few people want to listen to them. No crisis is ever exactly like the last one and the next great depression will be different from the last one. In the last depression those who had money were in a good financial position to ride it out but the next depression will see those with fiat money drowning in it as it becomes worthless. Very few Americans have any significant savings today. Most live on credit and those with savings have it stored in financial instruments that will be wiped out as the bankers collapse the system. Those who think they will retire with their IRA, pensions or Social Security will suddenly find them all gone never to return, leaving them with no means to care for themselves. All of the social safety nets that exist now to keep people fat and happy will fail.

"When the next great depression hits it will be unlike anything we have lived through before. Nothing will be as it seems and only those that have the resources to adapt will come through it whole. Preparation is the key to adapting to future events and those without resources will reap a bitter harvest as they struggle to survive. No announcements will be made, no warnings will be given by the establishment, it will just suddenly happen out of the blue and everyone will say it was unpredictable. But those who prepared will know better."

The worst feeling in the world comes when liquidity vanishes. When you must sell and you can't, then fear and anxiety replace the self-assurance and certainty of better days. Shrinking liquidity often escalates into panic. Liquidity can disappear in any market and requires major downward price adjustments. Prices simply evaporate and losses become unbearable. Panic selling overwhelms the market. David Stockman writes, "The house of cards is so shaky and so fragile right now that there is the risk of the proverbial black swan event. We don't see something coming. It shocks the system. It triggers a panic, and the panic soon envelops itself and descends into some sort of doom loop."

The late Richard Russell, editor of The Dow Theory Letter, talked about the bear luring in as many investors as possible before he strikes. The bear is out to destroy as much money as he can and he disguises his actions to fool people into thinking he is weak. He strikes when investors are most unsuspecting. The critical point comes when asset prices stop rising. Not a single credit and debt driven major asset bubble has ever ended in a soft landing. America's bubble economy is the worst in history. Heavily leveraged bonds running into the trillions comprise the mother of all bubbles. The current Federal Reserve tightening threatens to pull the rug out from this episode of excess. Be prepared for a relentless plunge in asset prices. And remember not much ammunition is left for monetary policy to reheat a dying speculative boom.

Here's the worst of all worlds following a market crash: Loans go into default, bankruptcies soar, stocks plummet further and losses mount. Wealth shrinks and prices of all assets erode. In the face of a great rush for liquidity, liquidity wanes. The small guy grits his teeth and weeps each morning as he reads the stock quotes. His relatives second-guess him to distraction. He constantly seeks reassurance from brokerage firm spokesmen on TV. Worry becomes a constant companion. He digs in and refuses to sell anything. His broker owns the same stocks and he agrees.

Large leverage players and international money management stars take a pounding. Assets under management shrivel and sophisticated money goes to the sidelines. Activity diminishes. Volume drops. Legions of burned investors sue. Unemployment mounts. Tax receipts fall and budget deficits grow. The government must return tax money for losses on stock transactions. Unemployment benefits and social costs cause greater government deficits. GDP shrinks and corporate profits erode. Massive layoffs cause civil disturbances and unrest. Leftists become media darlings. Government mortgage and loan guarantees require billions as failures and bankruptcies reach epidemic proportions. Runaway U.S. budget deficits require massive funding. Municipalities go broke.

The dollar takes a vicious drop. The Fed pushes interest rates lower and sinks the dollar further. Foreigners, gripped by a sickening downward spiral of domestic asset values, sell whatever is liquid and U.S. bonds go out the window. U.S. interest rates see-saw as dollar dumping gains impetus. Politicians and monetary officials make frequent reassurances and daily promises that are broken on the following day. Inflation accelerates and the people begin ridding themselves of dollars in exchange for tangible goods.

A wave of bankruptcies sweep financial service companies. Brokerages and management companies implode. Home values drop by a third or more. Loan and mortgage companies succumb. Credit card companies look to the government for a bailout. Small banks fail and big banks get round after round of government transfusions. Conditions worsen. The unthinkable happens. The U.S. government fails to fund certain programs and delays some major payments. Government guarantees on loans gone sour stack up unpaid. Decades of credit expansion disintegrate into a monumental debt collapse that threatens the solvency of the government. The economy is in ruins.

Make no mistake about it, a debt-driven consumption boom in conjunction with a credit-driven speculative boom can explode like a double-barreled shotgun next to your ear. Will it happen? Who knows? The point is that it can happen. It's in no way a remote possibility.

Virtually everyone holds their financial assets within a system that depends on outside circumstances for value. High stock prices depend on a continuing stream of new money and good business performance. Bonds depend on sound corporate finances. Treasury Bills depend on government solvency. Most of our nation's wealth lies within a government-nurtured system. Deposits are guaranteed and only mainstream investments are encouraged by the financial and political establishment. That's how they make their money. But all these assets depend on something else for their value. They don't stand alone. For the most part they are intertwined, all dependent on one another and backstopped by government insurance and guarantees.

Commercial real estate falls within this investment mainstream and home ownership has immense government financial support. But real estate values depend upon the effectiveness of government and central bank manipulation of the economy and in many cases government guarantees and supports. Real estate forms another part of the financial system that depends on outside economic factors for a good share of its value. Collectibles such as antiques and art don't depend on government or business solvency for value. However, they do depend on the general health of the economy. A depression can easily cause these items to plunge in value.

The one asset least affected by economic performance, business solvency, government guarantees, or insurance is gold. The yellow metal depends on no institution or government for value. Gold exists outside the mainstream and depends on none of the same things that stocks, bonds and banks depend on. Gold means independence. Gold allows the citizen to escape total reliance on the state-sponsored financial system. It's a perfect asset for ultimate protection, no matter how dicey things get. Gold's value may be affected by the U.S.'s economic performance, but far less than other assets. In fact, if the mainstream financial system breaks down gold goes up because people turn to gold in a crisis. Gold does best when everything else suffers.

Analyst Mark J. Lundeen gives this advice:"The key thing to keep in mind with holding gold and silver is that our world is heavily indebted by weak credit and rickety banks; and so is pregnant with counterparty risk. Gold and silver have no counterparty risks. The day is coming when trillions of dollars in flight capital are going to flee the deflating financial asset markets, and attempt to squeeze into the tiny gold and silver markets. I believe a day is coming when the price of gold and silver will rise to levels that are simply unbelievable to people today.

"Remember that at the beginning of the 20th century gold and silver were money. Paper money a hundred years ago was understood by all to be a debt payable in gold and silver bullion. This metallic monetary standard prevented the banking system from inflating the money supply, and it created economic stability in the marketplace and government finance that is totally missing today. But after two world wars, and a cold war with Communism, the old monetary metals were demonetized as central banks and politicians monetized the gullible belief in the full faith and credit of a central government. Of course central banks in our current monetary system have issued an excess of dollars, euros, and yen; they've issued more money than can ever fit into the tiny gold and silver markets in a financial panic."

Here's something else to worry about. Editor Simon Black tells us, "A few weeks ago the Board of Trustees of Social Security sent a formal letter to the United States Senate and House of Representatives to issue a dire warning: Social Security is running out of money. Given that tens of millions of Americans depend on this public pension program as their sole source of retirement income, you'd think this would have been front page news.

"But that didn't happen. The story was hardly picked up. It's astonishing how little attention this issue receives considering it will end up being one of the biggest financial crises in U.S. history. That's not hyperbole either – the numbers are very clear. The U.S. government itself calculates that the long-term Social Security shortfall exceeds $46 trillion. In other words, in order to be able to pay the benefits they've promised, Social Security needs a $46 trillion bailout. Fat chance. That amount is over twice the national debt, and nearly three times the size of the entire U.S. economy. Moreover, it's nearly sixty times the size of the bailout that the banking system received back in 2008. So this is a pretty big deal.

"This is a nationwide problem. Social Security is running out of money. State and local pension funds are running out of money. And even still their assumptions are wildly optimistic. So the problem is much worse than their already dismal forecasts."

Most people have their assets within the Wall Street – Washington financial axis. Many are totally dependent for retirement benefits and income from this alliance of government, business and central bank. It's where everybody keeps their money. That's because the people believe the government will always protect and take care of them. Of course the government wants to foster economic growth, prosperity, security and investment profits. But the government also takes strong measures to improve education, eliminate crime, improve race relations and eliminate poverty, to mention but a few of its notorious failures. In other words, the government's ineptitude and rank political motivations make the outcome of their insurance, influence and intervention in the markets unworthy of anyone's total trust and reliance for their financial security.

Analyst Egon von Greyerz writes, "Governments and central banks have mortgaged the future for generations to come. Nobody believes that this money will ever be repaid or that the liabilities can be met.

Thus, there will not be an orderly outcome of the greatest financial bubble in history." Author Doug Casey concludes, "The world economy is going to wind up crashed on the rocks. It's going to be very ugly. And soon."

CHAPTER XXVIII
A LITTLE PARANOIA IS GOOD

"Gold will be around, gold will be money when the dollar and the euro and the yuan and the ringgit are mere memories."

~ Richard Russell

Reports of police standing aside or not showing up in Oakland or Portland to protect the public from unruly left-wing demonstrators should cause great alarm. When the police excuse themselves from their duty because of politics or because they are union members we are all at risk. These communist extremists share Lenin's revolutionary enthusiasm. He would murder anybody that got in his way. Some of these demonstrators are so full of hate and righteousness they too would justify atrocities against the rich. If the cops don't come when you call them it's the end of America as we've known it.

The Reds thought nothing of killing people to advance their cause. The Marxists made great use of criminals who joined the party and helped butcher the well-to-do, the entrepreneurs and those who had assets. They thought nothing of robbing the safe deposit boxes in every bank in Russia. How many of today's demonstrators are of similar ilk? Enough to make me slightly paranoid about our future safety and security.

These are Lenin's children. What the Marxists have done in the past they can do again. In Russia they hated the free market in agriculture. So they murdered 7 million farmers. They shot them, stabbed them, burned them and hung them. They took the mothers, children, babies and grandparents on trains to Siberia and dumped them off in winter with nothing but the clothes on their back. In spring not a soul could be found.

Richard Ebeling explains, "As many as 200 million people have died as part of the dream of creating a collectivist 'Paradise on Earth.' A 'new world' was taken to mean the mass murder of all those that the socialist revolutionary leaders declared to be 'class enemies,' including the families, the children of 'enemies of the people.'

"A witness wrote in 1920: 'The machine of the Red Terror works incessantly. Every day and every night, in Petrograd, Moscow, and all over the country the mountain of the dead grows higher. Everywhere people are shot, mutilated, wiped out of existence.'

"This murderous madness never ended. In the 1930's, during the time of the Great Purges instituted by Soviet dictator Josef Stalin to wipe out all 'enemies of revolution' through mass executions, there were also millions sent to the Gulag prisons that stretched across all of the Soviet Union to be worked to death as slave labor to 'build socialism.' Before being sent to their death or to the forced labor camps, tens of thousands would be interrogated and cruelly tortured to get confessions out of people about non-existent crimes, imaginary anti-Soviet conspiracies, and false accusations against others."

When the farmers resisted they were shot or deported to slave labor camps. Starvation became a policy. Vast areas were robbed of their grain. Food shipments were not allowed to go to the hungry. In 1933, 25,000 people died of starvation every day. It was written, "The once smiling young faces of children vanished forever amid the constant pain of hunger. It gnawed away at their bellies, which became grossly swollen, while their arms and legs became like sticks as they slowly starved to death." Three million children perished.

The farmers were obliterated. Meanwhile the New York Times claimed all talk of famine was ridiculous. The Times admired the Soviet system. Their reporter won the Pulitzer Prize for his glowing reports on Russia. These days the Times probably doesn't see anything wrong with the police letting a radical leftist mob destroy private property. What happens if the dollar fails and the money is no longer there for welfare, unemployment, food stamps and other social schemes? How big will the demonstrations be and how dangerous? Will the police and the National Guard be influenced by radical politicians? Will the criminals be unleashed on the 1%?

Igor Shafarevich, author and prisoner in the Gulag wrote: "Most socialist doctrines and movements are literally saturated with the mood of death, catastrophe, and destruction. One could regard the death of mankind as the final result to which the development of socialism leads."

It's important to remember how ruthless and bloody socialists and statists have been. Nobody in Russia thought Lenin could prevail. The Czar and Czarina never dreamed that someday the Reds would herd their little family into a room and slaughter them. We have our share of collectivists and criminals in America who would do us harm. Backed by the "useful idiots" in the liberal party they could cause the ground beneath us to fall away. Keep this possibility in mind. If not for you, for your children and grandchildren. For them our fears should be ongoing. Our left wing political opponents are no strangers to a heritage of doing great evil in the name of good.

Author William Anderson writes, "The horrors of the Soviet invasion of Latvia, Estonia, and Lithuania in 1940 are long behind, surfacing only in the Museum of the Occupation, now located in the former U.S. embassy in downtown Riga.

"The Museum of the Occupation provides reminders of how the ancestors of people walking freely about the towns and cities of these countries suffered, and suffered greatly at the hands of those promoting the socialist ideology that even today won't die. How thousands were summarily executed at the hands of the NKVD, the Soviet secret police. How thousands more were herded into those tiny boxcars and shipped to the hinterlands of Siberia, many to die brutal deaths in labor camps. All because they were people who worked in government or taught in schools and universities of the Baltic nations, or who owned businesses, or who were just inconvenient to Soviet authorities. All on the ultimate order of Josef Stalin, the Soviet dictator called "Uncle Joe" by American journalists and by presidents Franklin Roosevelt and, later, Harry Truman.

"American publications like the New York Times were so in love with the ideals of the Bolshevik Revolution (and still are, given the NYT's series last year lamenting the fall of the Soviet Union and its Eastern Europe satellites) that they could not be bothered to tell the truth about what the communists did in the Baltics, just as they denied that Stalin had created a famine that killed more Ukranians than Jews that were killed in the Holocaust. Even now, as one looks at photos of the Baltic people being shot, arrested, buried in mass graves, and forced into labor camps, one is reminded that the Soviet Union did not provide a new way of living, as socialist apologists and American journalists have claimed, but rather just another way of dying – and dying violently.

"And, yet, there are people in high places in the U.S.A., those at the New York Times and elsewhere in the media and in academe that believe that communism had brought in a superior civilization. I recently saw a photograph of American Antifa protesters holding up a communist flag with the hammer-and-sickle and images of Mao, Lenin, and Marx. Perhaps they and the editors of the New York Times want to see the USA embrace a system that others that have lived under it now reject, and reject vehemently. Given that Antifa increasingly is providing shock troops for the causes espoused by prominent members of the Democratic Party like Bernie Sanders, the new drive for communism might not be as fringe as one might hope, and if a century of bloodshed, murder, vast prison systems, and starvation won't convince the advocates of communism among American millennials, then perhaps nothing will."

Author Paul Johnson: "The collapse of the Soviet Empire in 1989, laid bare the degree of devastation which the command economy, or socialism, or Communism, or whatever you care to call the Marxist-Leninist way of running things, has inflicted on the environment in Eastern Europe and West and Central Asia. We are only now beginning to understand the magnitude of the damage which has been done, some of it irreparable. The Soviet Union ruined the entire Aral Sea and some of the largest river systems in the world. What is notable is that the environmentalist lobbies, once so noisy in contrasting capitalist shame with socialist pride, have made no apology at all for thus misleading the world. They have simply passed to fresh battles, usually against Western governments and international companies."

The writer Humberto Fontova recently wrote this about the New York Times' love affair with another murderous dictator: "The past 10 days have seen three hysterical editorials from the New York Times pleading for a U.S. economic lifeline to the Castro brothers to end the so-called embargo.

"In April of 1959 – amidst an appalling bloodbath of Cubans by firing squad ordered by Fidel Castro but mostly administered by his ever-faithful Igor, Che Guevara – Castro made a special visit to the New York Times offices in New York. After a warm greeting from Arthur Hayes Sulzberger, a beaming Fidel Castro personally decorated a beaming Herbert Matthews [who interviewed Castro for the Times] with a specially-minted medal expressing his bloody regime's highest honor.

"'To our American friend Herbert Matthews with gratitude,' beamed Castro as the flashbulbs popped. 'Without your help, and without the help of the New York Times, the Revolution in Cuba would never have been.'

"'Fidel Castro has strong ideas of liberty, democracy and social justice,' Matthews had written on the front pages of the world's most prestigious newspaper in February 1957. Reasonable people might ask: has any tiny little thing transpired in the intervening half-century that might cause the New York Times to regret their enabling of Fidel Castro?

"But reasonable people will search in utter vain for any hint of such regret, especially in light of recent editorials, which – if anything – double down on the Times' historical fondness for the Castro regime. The New York Times enabled into power a regime that jailed and tortured political prisoners at a higher rate than Stalin's during the Great Terror."

Author Richard Baehr sums it up, "The true believers on the left say they want nothing more than equality and better lives for the masses, but communist equality has always meant equalizing the suffering, reducing living standards, and eliminating dissent or political opposition."

CHAPTER XXIX

CULTURE WARS

"It is the greenback which is unstable, and not bullion."
~ Dr. Franz Pick

The left has been politicizing its constituents for decades. They have been better at it because early on they captured the schools and the media. They control the institutions. From this vantage point they have initiated a culture war – a direct assault on the old values. Author David Gelernter writes, "The left owns American culture. Nearly every university, newspaper, TV network, Hollywood studio, publisher, school and museum in the nation. The left wrapped up the culture war two generations ago. Throughout my own adult lifetime, the right has never made one significant move against the liberal culture machine."

William Bennett tells us in the *The De-Valuing of America*, "Those whose beliefs govern our institutions will in large measure win the battle for the culture." He quotes Midge Decter, "A culture war, as the liberals understood far better than did their conservative opponents, is a war to the death. For a culture war is not battle over policy, though policy in many cases gives it expression; it is rather a battle about matters of the spirit."

Bennett continues, "So be it. Reclaiming our institutions is less a political opportunity than a civic obligation. It involves hard work. But it is work of immense importance. At the end of the day, somebody's values will prevail."

Often institutions of higher learning lead the assault on our values and culture. Colleges and universities have become the chief domain of the radical left. As author Les Csorba writes in *Academic License*, "The obvious result has been an assault on what we've traditionally called a 'liberal education.' The classical or great books of Western Civilization, which teach virtue, order and civility, and which lie as the political foundation of our constitutional republic have been attacked by academic disciples fostering new truly quasi-academic disciplines such as 'Peace Studies'…and so on." Shakespeare and Cervantes are replaced with obscure politically correct poets. Marxism, a miserable economic and social failure is alive and well within American universities.

Author John M. Ellis explains, "In most humanities and social science departments – especially those central to a liberal education, such as history, English and political science – the share of left-of-center faculty approaches 100%.

"The imbalance is not only a question of numbers. Well-balanced opposing views act as a corrective for each other: The weaker arguments of one side are pounced on and picked off by the other. Both remain consequently healthier and more intellectually viable. But intellectual dominance promotes stupidity. As one side becomes numerically stronger, its discipline weakens. The greater the imbalance between the two sides, the more incoherent and irrational the majority will become.

"What we are now seeing on the campuses illustrates this general principle perfectly. The nearly complete exclusion of one side has led to complete irrationality on the other. With almost no intellectual opponents remaining, campus radicals have lost the ability to engage with arguments and resort instead to the lazy alternative of name-calling: Opponents are all 'fascists,' 'racists' or 'white supremacists.' The campus radical monopoly on political ideas amounts to the shutting down of higher education as we have known it."

If you wonder why a simple prayer in school causes such a fuss, why quotas and affirmative action were stuffed down your throat, or why Columbus suddenly became a stinker; you can be sure it all started with the liberals at our universities. The left has made its mark. This is the age of excess. There's a boom in fun, self-indulgence and entertainment; endless examples of bad taste and vulgarity and shameless citizens sharing degrading personal revelations on TV. Roger Kimball writes, "At least since the sixties, the left-liberal consensus in America has worked to undermine traditional notions of decency, order, merit, and achievement."

Writing about the decay of the American character (and culture), commentator Charles J. Sykes explains, "Something extraordinary is happening in American society. Crisscrossed by invisible trip wires of emotional, racial, sexual and psychological grievance, American life is increasingly characterized by the plaintive insistence, I am a victim... the mantra of the victims is the same: I am not responsible, it's not my fault." The left has promoted massive subsidies that encourage this mindset. People believe they deserve something for nothing. They are victims. They rationalize a free ride. They are told the playing field isn't level, that merit is a scam, that values are subjective, that doing nothing is no better or worse than building and creating.

According to the author David Horowitz, "The left envisions a fundamentally transformed America, where the left's chief weapon is race. But even as progressives prosecute this race war, racial bigotry by whites has ceased to be a factor in public life. Progressives deal with this reality by inventing a fiction called 'institutional racism.' 'Institutional racism' is a necessary fiction because actual racists have become so hard to find. Even as white racism has become a phenomenon of the insignificant fringe the left's accusations of white racism have escalated to the point of terminal absurdity. Progressive voices describe America as a 'white supremacist nation.' This accusation is made against a country that outlaws racial discrimination that has twice elected a black president, has recently had a black four-star general head of the Joint Chiefs of Staff, two black secretaries of state, three black national security advisors and two successive black attorneys general along with thousands of black elected officials, mayors, police chiefs and congressmen."

Author and historian Victor David Hanson writes, "The United States has always cherished its 'melting pot' ethos of blending diverse peoples into one through assimilation, integration and intermarriage. When immigration was controlled, measured and coupled with a confident approach to assimilation, America thrived. Various ethnic groups enriched America with diverse art, food, music and literature while accepting a common culture of American values and institutions. Problems arose only when immigration was often illegal, in mass and without emphasis on assimilation.

"Sometime in the late 20th century, America largely gave up on multiracialism under one common culture and opted instead for multiculturalism, in which each particular ethnic group retained its tribal chauvinism and saw itself as separate from the whole. For those who see America becoming a multicultural state of unassimilated tribes and competing racial groups, history will not be kind. The history of state multiculturalism is one of discord, violence, chaos and implosion."

Nonie Darwish, human rights actiivist, explains how the left is warping our culture for immigrants. "As a young woman, I accomplished my dream of moving to America in November of 1978. America was my outlet to freedom, economic self-reliance and escape from being surrounded by misery, injustice and poverty. I knew that if I worked hard in America I would achieve success, and I did.

"Left on their own, immigrants are grateful to work hard and enjoy the American system, but soon after we are here, we are told by the popular culture that we are victims, must act like ones, and we must not accept what America can offer. We are told that the system is rigged, not fair and that 'whites' who have welcomed us in the millions for centuries, are racists and bigoted. Many immigrants believed the anti-American propaganda for the sake of approval and benefits. Immigrants are now told to hold on to their old culture, religion, traditional clothes, customs, language, and even some of the archaic laws, which many have escaped from in the first place. The conventional wisdom now tells us that America is no better than the oppressive systems we originally came from.

"In America today, every national origin and race is encouraged to find a minority group to belong to. When I first moved to America, no Muslim women wore the Islamic garb, and you could hardly tell on the streets of America who was Muslim and who was not. Now many Muslims find power in sticking together, and go back to the Islamic garb and cry victimization. When I privately once asked a Muslim professor why she started wearing the head cover in America, her answer was a whisper: 'The ethnic look is powerful in America.'

"Immigrants in America today are faced with a dilemma; they must deny their appreciation of the capitalist system that brought them here in the first place. Their children are taught to reject their parents' experience of hard work to get ahead and regard their parents as victims of discrimination and abuse. They are rewarded for complaining and rejecting assimilation, free enterprise, self-reliance, and appreciation of American values that made this country the envy of the world."

One thing that worries me is the increasing politicization of criminals. The left is endangering us all with their accusations and blame that stirs up hatred. Criminals would have no compunction against ignoring the Constitution. They could easily unite with radicals on the left to take extreme measures against successful people. Communist revolutionaries have often used criminals to murder business people and capitalists. An expanding welfare system leads to more bad actors. So far riots and arson have been limited to minority neighborhoods. However, the level of hatred has been amped up by community organizers and other radicals. We hear a constant refrain that old white guys are racist and have all the money. Supposedly, successful people are responsible for inequality and unfairness. Politics and crime make a volatile and dangerous mix. It puts the barbarians inside the gates. It divides the country like nothing else. The left constantly tears the scab off old wounds and raises issues that distort reality and nurse hard feelings. Inciting political hate is a dangerous trend that leads to attacking people for political reasons. It's the poison that leads to atrocities and crimes against innocent people.

Dennis Prager claims, "America has become the least racist multiracial, multiethnic country in world history." A letter to the Wall Street Journal editorial page from a thankful African immigrant bears this out, "I grew up in the Congo and have numerous friends in the U.S. from the Congo and other African countries who are here for an education or a better life. Every one of them is grateful for the opportunity to secure an excellent education. The U.S. offers the opportunity to pursue their dreams and a chance to raise their families in peace. Most come here from different cultures with minimal money and limited English language skills. Interestingly, I've never heard one complain about discrimination, obstacles or being a victim. Rather, they are grateful."

The left would be quick to brand me as a racist because I'm a libertarian and a conservative. Anglo Saxons with my views are supposedly white supremacists, bigots, and prejudiced towards minorities. However, I don't believe the black people I have helped think I'm a racist. In 1984, I paid to bring two groups of six kids from Ethiopia to get their hearts fixed. The necessary surgery was too complicated for Ethiopian hospitals. They were weak and sick when they arrived and the prognosis was not good. Ten days after their surgery they were racing around the hospital and bouncing off the walls. They were beautiful kids. Before they went back to Ethiopia, my wife and I took them to Toys-R-Us and let them buy two toys to take home with them.

However, one ten-year-old boy could not go back. He needed a pacemaker, and they did not have the technology in Ethiopia to periodically check it. When asked what he would like to do he said, "I'd like to live with the Cooks." Consequently, we took him into our home and eventually adopted him. When he grew up, he married a lovely girl from Eritrea (a country boarding Ethiopia). Her father was a senior airline mechanic for Northwest Airlines. The family had fled Ethiopia after being persecuted by the communist dictator Mengistu. Our payoff is that we now have two beautiful granddaughters, 10 and 12, who are excelling in school. I give them $5 for every A they get on their report cards, and they don't hesitate to let me know what I owe them.

Naturally, I got to know some other Ethiopian people that live in Minnesota. The other day, when I was getting off the plane in Minneapolis, one of the workers grabbed me and gave me a hug. A few years ago, we helped him get his young son here and reunited the family. All of the Ethiopians I have met have jobs and are successful. Among them are entrepreneurs and professionals. They appreciate America and the opportunity it gave them for a better life.

CHAPTER XXX
PENALTY ON PROGRESS

*"Bullion doesn't pay interest or dividends, nor does it grow
or expand by itself. That's the price you pay for tranquility."*
~ Pierre Lassonde

In the winter I spend some time on a little island in southwest
Florida. This tropical paradise runs seven miles long and is two
blocks wide. A small toll bridge connects it to the mainland.
For the most part, the four thousand residents (in peak season) are
wealthy. One or two are in the Forbes 400.

Every morning a constant stream of autos and trucks cross onto the
island. They contain people who work on the homes and the yards
of the affluent. This constant flow of carpenters, maids, plumbers,
landscapers, air conditioning contractors, handymen, pool clean-
ers, security guards, repairmen, cable guys, gardeners and decora-
tors make their livelihood off the rich. When taxes are raised on the
wealthy, fewer of these workers will be employed.

The late economist, Murray Rothbard, had this to say about the dangers of tax gouging. "The modern welfare state, highly touted as soak-
ing the rich to subsidize the poor, does no such thing. In fact, soak-
ing the rich would have disastrous effects, not just for the rich but for
the poor and middle class themselves. For it is the rich who provide a
proportionately greater amount of saving, investment capital, entre-
preneurial foresight, and financing of technological innovation, that
has brought the United States to by far the highest standard of living
– for the mass of the people – of any country in history."

Rich people and people attempting to get rich create the jobs. Unemployment will rise when taxes are increased. If you want to impoverish the populace of a country, tax the rich out of existence. In that
way you can turn the country into a third world hellhole. There are
few millionaires in Bangladesh or similar economic backwaters. The
more millionaires and billionaires in a country, the higher the stan-

dard of living. All the former communist countries have learned this lesson. They continue to push tax rates lower towards 10%. Their economies are growing. Eventually their standard of living could someday pass ours.

Our liberals and progressives want to raise taxes and pass out money to alleviate income inequality. Unfortunately, this redistribution scheme does just the opposite. It makes everybody worse off. Taking money from those who earned it for the government to waste on a myriad of follies reduces our national wealth and prosperity.

The emotional mix of envy and altruism, which comprises modern liberalism, pays no heed to century-old lessons of economics. Rather, it relies on socialist misconceptions. The liberal tax agenda is the harbinger of economic retrogression and national failure. Every citizen at every economic level will suffer because of it.

A few years ago, the exceedingly liberal Minneapolis newspaper ran an editorial on baseball. They referred to Yankee owner, George Steinbrener (1930-2010), as greedy. More recently, one sport columnist called Dallas Cowboys owner Jerry Jones greedy because he wanted to add more games to the season schedule. That sounds more like a good business move. Liberals love to describe successful people as greedy. They prefer the type of business person personified by Wesley Mouch, a character in Ayn Rand's novel, *Atlas Shrugged*. Mr. Mouch was proud of the fact that his heavily subsidized company had never made a profit.

When George Steinbrener ran the Yankees he did what was necessary to win. He built an entertaining team and the fans reward him with a profit. Baseball salaries may be out of the park, but blame much of that on inflation, players unions and agents. You don't have to love the Yankees, but you have to admire their success over the years. George fielded a winner and filled the ballpark. Wasn't that his job? As for Jerry Jones, he built a storied franchise known as "America's Team." He should be lauded for his great accomplishment.

Virtually anyone who makes a lot of money gets written off by the left as greed-driven. Most of the animosity stems from envy. The sight of people who have made money through greater ability bothers them. They credit this solely to luck, dishonesty or greed. They forget that under the market system you acquire wealth by serving others. Everyone has the same opportunity under capitalism and most of us start from the same place. Those with the ability to provide products and services to the greatest number of people make the most money.

Editorial writers for liberal newspapers don't fare as well at money making as high-tech innovators. However, they prefer to believe that this income disparity comes through exploitation or luck. They want to believe that someone goes without because someone else gets rich. They root for higher taxes to level incomes. But the money earned by wealthy entrepreneurs does not cause anyone's poverty. The same process that makes entrepreneurs rich also satisfies the people's wants and needs in the best and cheapest way. Business standardizes our consumption and enjoyment and every citizen shares in these material blessings.

Envy and ignorance of how free market capitalism works account for both the Leninists of yesterday and the liberals of today. Their animosity towards profit-making has saddled business with a host of regulations and social requirements that competitors in other parts of the world don't have to deal with. Liberals love government and its multiple cures for every social ailment. They fail to realize that public social programs exhaust the resources of the nation and corrupt the citizenry.

Sad to say, I have friends, and even relatives, who vote for political candidates on the left. Generally, they have embraced liberalism because of one or more social issues that concern them. Unfortunately, they allow this narrow perspective to override the great historical struggle of our time between socialism and capitalism (free market vs. government control). They erroneously believe this conflict to be irrelevant or no longer germane. For this belief, they risk exchanging their prosperity and freedom for poverty and statism.

Hostility towards business runs deep on the left. On college campuses professors pontificate about robber-barons and corporate crooks. Their heroes are never business pioneers or innovative entrepreneurs. They would rather enshrine a Che Guevara than a Ray Kroc or Tom Watson. Che, that hero of leftist lore once claimed, "The oppressor must be killed mercilessly...the revolutionary must become an efficient and selective killing machine." Contrast that with a capitalist hero of today, George Gilder, who said, "Do unto others as you would have them do unto you, and "Give and you will be given unto," are the central rules of the life of enterprise."

Support for the left means far more than promoting your personal social cause. It's a vote for high taxes, big government, overregulation, statism and less freedom. It's a vote for the government to take more and more of what people earn. As much as anything, it's a vote to put all commerce under the thumb of politicians and government to the point they die off like so many dinosaurs. Voting for a liberal may keep your social cause alive and well, but if the left gains enough influence, you are going to hate your low wages, empty shelves and old car.

Private business and entrepreneurs make much better use of their profits than government. Bureaucrats can't introduce new products and services, create jobs or wealth. Every dollar taxed off by government hurts economic growth. High taxes are a penalty on progress. Low taxes spur growth. The fastest growing economy in Europe is Albania with a 10% tax rate. Texas, with no state income tax, was recently creating 45% of the new jobs in America. There is no known example of higher taxes improving an economy. However, lowering taxes invariably increases prosperity.

It's a fabrication to claim that high income earners do not pay their fair share. There is no escaping the requirement to pay 42% of ordinary income to the government. In some states you can add another 10%. By historical standards this is punitive. It's close to the highest in the world. High taxes erode charity. The generosity of the American people is legendary. Now charitable acts are taken over and directed by the government.

Philosopher Andrew Galambos (1924-1977) wrote, "People who make more are taxed more. That's being punished for being more productive. And then you're being rewarded for being a parasite. If you don't do anything, if you're just a bum, why, you can go on relief. You get something for nothing. That's a violation of rationality and morality in the short run too. The less you do, the more you get. The more you do, the more you're punished. That's a fine standard for a culture! The most productive people are punished the most for being productive; the ones who produce the least are rewarded for being parasites. Now, if I tried to design an irrational structure of a society, this is exactly what I'd pick."

There is a moral issue. Why does someone who is down on his luck have a right to the earnings of others? What moral right does a subsidized business have to my money? Isn't it wrong for one person to benefit at the expense of another? Helping people should be a voluntary act free of government coercion.

Business has its ups and downs. High taxes make it difficult for a company to build cash reserves. Without this cushion in downturns more companies go out of business. The government has eroded their staying power and thereby increased unemployment. We used to have a socialist professor at the University of Minnesota who gained notoriety with his anti-business tirades. One day there was a demonstration that pitted his advocates against a handful of business people. In the verbal exchange that followed, one guy kept yelling "You've never made a payroll!" Frankly, I didn't get it. What the heck did he mean? What did making a payroll have to do with anything?

Years later, after I started my own business, I got it. For twenty years, from 1973 to 1993, four years were good and sixteen years were bad. When I had to go around to my employees and ask them if they could wait another two weeks before they got paid, I got it. When I went for months without a paycheck, I got it. When I laid off dozens of employees because business was bad, I got it. When I sold off my personal assets and the collection I loved to make payroll, I got it. When I cut us down to four-day weeks, I got it. When I laid awake a hundred nights racked by anxiety about how to make payroll, I got it.

The politicians, the media, the Hollywood liberals; they get it least of all. Our worldly goods, our luxuries, our services and our wealth don't come through osmosis. Somebody had to take a big risk, struggle against overwhelming odds, work long hours, go the extra mile, practice unstinting integrity and develop abiding faith. Most who try don't make it. Only by serving others better than the competition, or through innovation and new products can they succeed.

I'm not Hank Reardon or Midas Mulligan (*Atlas Shrugged*) but I can tell you that only the smallest number of individuals conceive the industrial and technological breakthroughs that dramatically improve our living standards. One such person was Henry Ford. In my book *The Start-up Entrepreneur* I wrote, "In 1914, he shocked the world as no man had ever before him. He doubled the wages of his workers…and reduced their hours…. The 'five-dollar day' stands out as one of the most generous acts in the history of commerce."

Nevertheless, Ford was forced to yield to Walter Reuther and the United Auto Workers in the 1930s. The New York Times called him "an industrial fascist." In the name of "social justice" Franklin Roosevelt sanctioned unions and gave them broad powers. This, coupled with an overabundance of regulation and high taxes led to the decline of our automobile industry.

For profitable companies and big earners reducing taxes becomes an obsession. Too much time is wasted on this exercise, deductions are stretched, and unworkable tax shelters are sometimes employed. It takes hard work and struggle to make a profit. Nevertheless, the tax system punishes successful, productive people and rewards those who are unproductive. No nation can prosper for long with such perverse incentives. Yes, a certain level of taxes are necessary but a high tax regime is misguided, unfair and counterproductive.

CHAPTER XXXI
THE APPROACHING CALAMITY

"How rare is gold? If you could gather together all the gold mined in recorded history, melt it down, and pour it into one giant cube, it would measure only about eighteen yards across! That's all the gold owned by every government on earth, plus all the gold in private hands, all the gold in rings, necklaces, chains, and gold art. That's all the gold used in tooth fillings, in electronics, in coins and bars. It's everything that exists above ground now, or since man learned to extract the metal from the earth. All of it can fit into one block the size of a single house. It would weigh about 91,000 tons – less than the amount of steel made around the world in an hour. That's rare."

~ Daniel M. Kehrer

I wish my old friend Kurt Richebächer was still alive. He could analyze financial data like no other. His warnings about the future would resonate today. Kurt was born in Germany in 1918. He grew up in the Hitler era. Kurt came to Minneapolis in 1994 and stayed at my home for a few days. I asked him about the war years in Germany. He was in the Wehrmacht. He completed basic training in 1941 and his unit was sent to the Russian front. A few days before they left he came down with a virus that paralyzed his legs. It might have been polio. He was hospitalized for months. The rest of his unit went to Russia and they were decimated. Most of his friends were killed. He told me that had he gone he never would have made it back to Germany.

After the war he returned to Berlin and earned a doctorate in economics. In 1964, he became chief economist and managing director of the Dresdner Bank. His rock-ribbed stance on money and credit excess earned him the plaudits of Paul Volcker and John Exter. Sometime in the 1980s he moved to the south of France and began a monthly report called the Richebächer Letter. He was interviewed in a newsletter and when I read it I thought this guy thinks just like me. Believe me, at the time, kindred spirits were hard to find. I called him and introduced myself. Thereafter, we talked once or twice a month until he died in 2007 at age 89.

What would Kurt have to say about today's monetary shenanigans? In 1999 he wrote, "The U.S. financial system today hangs in an increasingly precarious position, a house of cards literally built on nothing but financial leverage, speculation and derivatives." Today he would be apoplectic. He would shout over the phone to me that our financial engineering and Federal Reserve debt monetization are economic sins that dwarf anything in the past.

As far back as 1996 he was warning about a stock market crash. "The bullish wave threatens to come crashing down on the hordes of analysts and investors who bet so heavily – and so foolishly – on their dreams of a perpetual 'stock market boom." As the Nasdaq bubble deflated he wrote in June of 2000, "The decisive cause of every single, serious economic and currency crisis are credit and debt excesses. Apparently, we cannot repeat it often enough: the U.S. credit and debt excesses of the past few years are beyond past experience in history, essentially leaving behind a totally vulnerable economy and financial system."

One of his sternest warnings came in 1999 when he criticized Alan Greenspan for his speech endorsing derivatives. "To be the leading central banker of the world, it really ought to be obvious that the overriding consequences of widespread derivatives use is excessive leverage and risk-taking...derivatives markets encourage a dangerous shifting of risk to parties with less wherewithal to shoulder potential losses. This is particularly the case during an acute financial crisis precisely when derivative 'insurance' is called for. We see... massive shifting of market risk to the highly leveraged and exposed U.S. banking industry and Wall Street firms."

In 2002 he warned about the collapse of national savings: "The total carnage of national savings is the U.S. economy's most important – but also most widely ignored predicament...national savings have been squandered to pay for spending that the consumer cannot afford from his current income."

He continued with a crucial economics lesson, one that the Keynesians have totally failed to grasp. "Ever since Adam Smith, savings has meant exactly one and the same thing in all languages: it is the part of current income that is not spent on consumption. And the key point of this definition is that such savings, and such savings only, make it possible to divert real resources from the production of consumption goods to the production of capital goods.

"To pin down and emphasize the key point: savings from current income represent the economy's supply of capital. Thus, it definitely sets the limits to the financial funds and the real resources that are available for new capital investment. Any increase in consumer spending as a share of GDP correspondingly decreases the economy's capacity for capital formation. It is, of course, easy to replace missing savings with credit creation. But there is no substitute for missing real resources.

"In the end it is all about capital investment. It is the critical mass in the process of economic growth that generates all the things that make for rising wealth and living standards. Capital investment creates demand, growing supply, employment, productivity, income, profits and tangible wealth."

He concluded, "The crucial thing to see about the U.S. economy is that its growth during the past few years was driven by uncontrolled debt creation for consumption and financial speculation, while in the process domestic savings and the potential for capital investment have been devastated as never before.... The first thing to get straight is that this was – and still is – the most outrageous bubble economy in history, far worse than the U.S. bubble of the 1920s and Japan's bubble of the late 1980s." (Remember, this was 2002.)

Recall what Melchior Palyi said about the 1920s in the United States: "It was, indeed, an illiquid over-expanded colossus of debts, rather than an excessive money supply, on which the price structure of the 1920s rested."

"That is precisely our opinion about the U.S. economy and its financial system today. For us, the source of liquidity is all-important.

True liquidity comes from a surplus of income over spending; that is, from savings. False liquidity comes from borrowing. In a country with zero savings, all liquidity is essentially from borrowing. Nor is it a secret that it generally comes about through borrowing against rising asset prices."

"Very few people so far have realized that the U.S. economy is sick to the bone. In the past few years it has been grossly mismanaged, on the macro level through unprecedented monetary looseness on the part of the Greenspan Fed, and on the micro level through corporate strategies that built only mountains of financial leveraging but no factories."

In 2005, he delivered this indictment of the U.S. economy. "The ongoing credit explosion is financing a lot of different things, except production and tangible capital formation. Debt growth is almost entirely used for unproductive purposes, such as consumption, imports, government deficits, purchases of existing assets and financial speculation."

He continued, "Credit growth in the United States has gone completely insane. This is sheer Ponzi financing – and like all Ponzi schemes someone will end up holding the bag. At the same time, the diversion of credit into bonds, stock and housing has created an illusion of bulging wealth.

"This so-called wealth creation has its quack origins in loose money and artificially low interest rates; it boosts consumption at the expense of saving and investment. Strictly speaking, this is the exact opposite of wealth creation – impoverishment."

By 2006 Kurt Richebächer was warning about an impending downturn. "The U.S. economy is in danger of a recession that will prove unusually severe and long.... The great question is what will happen to the variety of financial asset bubbles in the United States when the housing bubble bursts and the economy slumps."

Kurt Richebächer was a deflationist at heart. He wrote, "Asset price inflation is self-financing because it creates the rising collateral for the borrowing that propels prices higher. With reckless bankers and borrowers, this can go to extremes. Yet there is an inexorable end. And this means over-indebted borrowers have to sell their collateralized assets, driving down their prices.

"What is debt deflation? To quote Irving Fisher, who analyzed the debt deflation of the 1930s: 'The very effort of individuals to lessen their burden of debt by selling assets increases it because of the mass effect of the stampede to liquidate in swelling each dollar owed.' In other words, heavy asset selling drives down asset prices, which drives up indebtedness. To quote Mr. Fisher again: 'Then we have the great paradox which, I submit, is the chief secret of all great depressions: The more the debtors pay [by selling their assets], the more they owe.'

"Thus, over-investment and over-speculation are often important; but they would have far less serious results were they not conducted with borrowed money. The same is true of overconfidence. I fancy that overconfidence seldom does any great harm except when, as and if it beguiles its victims into debt.

"Mr. Fisher lost his total fortune in the stock market crash. He was America's great apostle in the 1920s, who had preached that the stable price level in consumer and producer prices over the decade reflected and guaranteed a healthy economy and healthy markets. Belatedly, he discovered that insane borrowing had driven the stock market's bull run. From this late recognition, he developed his debt-deflation theory."

In the spring of 2007 Kurt Richebächer suddenly lost his eyesight. In our last conversation I could hear the anguish in his voice as he explained to me that he had gone permanently blind. To someone who spent much of their time reading financial reports and economic statistics this was devastating beyond measure. Soon afterwards Kurt Richebächer passed away.

In one of his final newsletters in January of 2007 he wrote with amazing prescience, "In our view, the obvious major risk is in the impending bust of the gigantic housing bubble. Home ownership is broadly spread among the population, in contrast to owning stocks. So the breaking of the housing bubble will hurt the American people far more than did the collapse in stock prices in 2000 – 2002…. Someday, the same will happen to the bond and stock market…. Another big risk is the dollar."

It's sad that Kurt Richebächer did not live to see the sorry outcome of the monetary excesses he warned about. The accuracy of his predictions makes him the soothsayer of the century. The economist Paul Krugman argued in 2002 that the Federal Reserve should do what it could to create a housing bubble; yet, he received a Nobel Prize. Nobody paid much attention to Kurt Richebächer and his accurate forecasts. In a rational world Kurt Richebächer would have won the Nobel and Krugman would have been fired.

Were he alive I'm sure Kurt Richebächer would agree with my view that Paul Krugman, from his influential post at the New York Times is the most dangerous and wrong-thinking economist since Karl Marx. Kurt would also have pilloried Mr. Bernanke and Janet Yellen just as he did Mr. Greenspan. He would argue that the politicians and monetary authorities in charge today suffer a profound economic ignorance. He would agree, they are leading us into catastrophe. He would be warning us about a falling dollar, a bursting bond bubble, a gathering recession and wrong-headed policy prescriptions coming from Washington.

CHAPTER XXXII
A FULL-BLOWN ECONOMIC COLLAPSE

"Civilization can only revive when there shall come into being in a number of individuals a new tone of mind independent of the one prevalent among the crowd and in opposition to it. A new public opinion must be created privately and unobtrusively. The existing one is maintained by the press, by propaganda, by organization, and by financial influences which are at its disposal The unnatural way of spreading ideas must be opposed by the natural one, which goes from man to man and relies solely on the truth of the thoughts and the hearer's receptiveness for new truth."

~ Albert Schweitzer

People cannot foresee the things they don't want to happen. In other words, your interest and need for some other outcome make it unlikely you will be ready for an economic shock. It's human nature. No matter how inevitable it may be, most people won't see a crash coming. Because the full fury of a market and currency collapse will strike unexpectedly you stand to be devastated by it. Every paper asset you own, everything you count on, and everything that has been promised you for your retirement can be swept away. In the long economic history of the world, no nation's economy or paper money has escaped the pitiless repudiations, failures, depressions, shocks, devaluations, hyper-inflations and bankruptcies that have wiped out the gullible citizenry. The 2008 crisis was only a warm-up for the main event.

For many years, various soothsayers have issued warnings of a serious economic collapse. So far they have proven to be wrong. Many people use this as a reason to scoff at such warnings. Because no devastating economic crisis has afflicted us in recent memory does not mean that such an event can't occur. In fact, the reasons these warnings were issued remain very much intact, and, in all cases, are more serious than before. The day of reckoning may have been postponed but it only has served to compound the problem. Author Harry Dent writes, "Bubbles always burst; there are no exceptions. The greater that bubble is, the greater it's going to burst! Financial bubbles tend to get more extreme over time, as the available credit that fuels them expands as our incomes and wealth expand. Bubbles become so attractive that eventually they suck in even the skeptics. No one wants the 'high' and easy gains to end, so we go into denial as the bubble evolves, especially in its latter stages."

The U.S. emphasizes consuming over saving. We are the grasshoppers fiddling away the summer while elsewhere the ants save and invest. This policy of eating the seed corn was promoted by liberal economists. Michael Snyder writes, "Today, we are living in the terminal phase of the biggest debt bubble in the history of the planet. Every debt bubble eventually ends tragically, and this one will too. Bill Gross recently noted that 'our highly levered financial system is like a truckload of nitroglycerin on a bumpy road.' One wrong move and the whole thing could blow sky high."

Editor Lance Roberts tells us, "Debt is, by its very nature, a cancer on economic growth. As debt levels rise it consumes more capital by diverting it from productive investments into debt service. As debt levels spread through the system it consumes greater amounts of capital until it eventually kills the host.

"The reality is that the majority of the aggregate growth in the economy since 1980 has been financed by deficit spending, credit creation and a reduction in savings. This reduced productive investment and the output of the economy slowed. As the economy slowed and wages fell consumers were forced to take on more leverage to maintain their standard of living which in turn decreased savings. As a result of the increased leverage more of their income was needed to service the debt – and with that, the "debt cancer" engulfed the system. Ineffective central bank policies, which cause interest rates to remain too low for too long, resulted in excessive credit creation, speculative economic bubbles and lowered savings."

Ralph Waldo Emerson wrote, "Fear is an instructor of great sagacity.... He indicates great wrongs that must be revised." The great wrong in our modern era was to give the government monopoly control over our money. The government's unlimited expansion of money and credit fosters the boom and bust business cycle. The reason to fear is that we are due for a bust. The coming panic and crash will dishearten the nation and show our politicians and monetary authorities to be seriously mistaken. We will suffer because of the great Keynesian error foisted upon us by Washington and Wall Street. This was the very warning written by the economists of the Austrian School.

Artificially low interest rates and boundless money and credit cause an unhealthy boom within which malinvestment and speculation flourish. Such a boom cannot last and must always lead to a slump and depression. In this current go-around, our monetary excesses created extremes in financialization, leverage and an asset boom. The Austrian School teaches that in the bubble economy unless money and credit continually expand, a slowdown occurs. More money is required or the crisis deepens. Our central bank has been pumping furiously for years, but recently this has come to a halt. As liquidity dries up the dogmatic Keynesians will once again press for money creation on a grand scale. That policy threatens the primacy of the dollar. Peter Schiff writes, "There's no way out of this box. There is no normalization of rates that is ever going to happen. The balance sheet is going to grow permanently, which means banana republic debt monetization. We just print money to finance government spending, which is going to explode."

Ludwig von Mises warned, "The monetary and credit policies of all nations are headed for a new catastrophe probably more disastrous than any of the prior slumps." You either take your medicine and let a depression kill off the excesses and mistakes in your economy or you ultimately hyperinflate and kill your currency. Dark days lie ahead. Our debts, wasteful spending, high taxes, overregulation and our welfare culture have deprived our economy of resilience. A bloated government smothers our vitality. There is no middle road out of this mess – "A great wrong must be revised." Sound money must resurface.

Egon von Greyerz warns, "We have false money – money which is fabricated by central banks and commercial banks. This money has zero intrinsic value and is backed by nothing, zilch, nada! So governments and individuals have spent money that doesn't exist. This is why the world is sitting on a debt mountain including derivatives of around $2.5 quadrillion. The world is now facing the risk of a total breakdown of the world economy and the financial system.

"As the financial system implodes, there will initially be unlimited money printing by central banks, but this time it will have no effect. The world will finally realize that creating wealth by putting ink on pieces of paper, or pressing a button to fabricate trillions of dollars or euros is a massive fraud. This fraud has been going on for most of the last 100 years but ordinary people will soon learn the hard way how governments have ruined their lives and the world economy.

"The current fragile state of the world and the dire consequences of the coming breakdown will never be printed in a newspaper, nor discussed on television. Ordinary people, indoctrinated by governments and the media are as bullish today as they were in 1929 before the crash or the crashes of 1973, 1987, 2000 or 2007. Nobody understands that the world is facing insurmountable problems that can no longer be repaired by corrupt hocus-pocus wizardry. Virtually nobody will prepare for the imminent collapse. This is because neither the so-called experts, nor ordinary people can see or understand the risks. Then there is also the belief that governments will save the world once more by flooding it with printed money."

Gloomy financial trends can't be brushed aside. Our economic sins are real. They defy ready solutions. Consequently, you can lose enormously on your paper assets. Your retirement and savings plans can be devastated. The government can be overwhelmed trying to cover guarantees and losses, to say nothing of trying to solve its own debt and currency problems. What passes for economic normalcy in America today is folly. Once it begins to unravel in earnest and the monetary authorities lose control, then comes panic. Only a few can see the dry rot undermining our financial affairs. People cannot foresee the things they don't want to happen.

Editor Fred Hickey writes, "Instead of letting economic nature take its course – recessions clearing excesses, fluctuating interest rates adjusting the price (and thus the quantity) of money, etc., the hubristic central bankers decided that since their intelligence was so wondrous, they could do a better job controlling the markets – central planning style. So the Fed and their central banker brethren around the globe determined that the world needed some extra money to make it work better. And when that (of course) didn't work, they doubled down with their quantitative easings and then doubled down again, and again. The end result is a world insanely flooded with excess liquidity and an economic system so warped and distorted we'll only be able to assess the economic damage caused by all the excesses after the floodwaters recede."

An economic earthquake will hurt those people the worst who can't afford to lose. More than ever you need to consider how to protect yourself. Gold is the only asset that protects you from virtually every economic danger. You need gold. It can save you. At a minimum put 10% of your net worth into gold. In light of the current problems I urge you to think about putting another 10% into silver. Present economic dangers suggest the bottom could fall out of other assets and markets at any time. You have little to lose. In five, 10 or 20 years the historical evidence argues that you will be able to sell your gold and get back at least what you put into it in terms of purchasing power.

CHAPTER XXXIII
THE ROLE OF GOLD

"Gold is forever. It is beautiful, useful, and never wears out. Small wonder that gold has been prized over all else, in all ages, as a store of value that will survive the travails of life and the ravages of time."

~ James Blakeley

Only a few commodities have true worldwide followings. The widespread international market for gold provides a degree of liquidity that renders gold less susceptible to any single nation's financial problems. That's why gold may be impervious to the same kinds of market drops that can affect stocks and other assets.

Gold doesn't bear interest because gold represents capital that has lower risk. It can't be affected by a bank failure, a market crash or a corporate bankruptcy. It can be argued that buying gold for possession in a relatively calm market is the most conservative investment possible and consequently the safest. Unfortunately, bouts of frantic trading in the highly leveraged futures market can detract from the safety of gold and make the timing of a purchase crucial. (With commodity futures buyers borrow most of the money for the purchase. It's risky, and it adds price volatility.)

Another fly in the gold ointment could be the 1,118 million ounces of gold held by central banks. This represents approximately 1/3 of the above ground supply. Another 1/3 exists in gold jewelry and 1/3 is held by investors. Some central banks have sold their gold. A desire for yields and more flexible reserves could spark additional central bank selling. Nonchalance and an utter disregard for the role of gold among younger economists and bankers may also encourage selling over the longer term. Future central bank sales, however, will be tempered by a reluctance to damage the price of gold and hurt the value of their holdings. Then there is the possibility of angering their citizenry and uncertainty about the future role of gold in monetary affairs.

With the exception of 1980 and 2011, an investment in the yellow metal has essentially kept its value in terms of purchasing power. If you bought gold in 1994, two decades later in 2014, you would still have a high value asset. Twenty years hence, you can be reasonably assured this value will still be there. You can't say that about much else.

Gold represents the purest form of wealth, the elemental basis of riches, the absolute among assets. Because of its international recognition and demand, its liquidity surpasses that of any other asset. Whether in Tashkent or Timbuktu, a half-ounce of gold in your hand means the same thing to everyone.

Certain assets such as diamonds, rare stamps, or collectibles require expertise and may be affected by subjectivity or fads. The value of the U.S. dollar can be eroded by inflation or by currency markets. Banks and bank accounts depend on interest rate fluctuations, and the financial strength of banking institutions, governments, insurers, and guarantors. Stocks are inherently unstable, dependent on individual company performance, and the confidence of the crowd. None of these things affect gold. At any one time on this earth, a majority of the billions of inhabitants have, in the back of their mind, a hope, a wish, or a plan, to acquire more gold. China and India have the world's largest populations and they are avid buyers of gold.

Gold futures, gold stocks, or gold options don't fill the bill for most of the world's gold buyers. They want gold in their physical possession. These indirect methods of owning gold have their place but carry greater levels of risk and astute timing requirements. They are fluid while gold is solid. For example, in an extended stock market crash, gold stocks could decline while gold prices rise.

No person of means should be without some gold in his or her possession. In this country we have had the best of what the world has had to offer for as long as any of us can remember. This in itself is unusual. History offers too many pessimistic examples of the worst of all worlds. We prospered in America for a specific set of reasons.

Virtually every person can add up their net worth in a few seconds. A minimum of 5% of this figure should be held in physical gold. This pure form of wealth can backstop all other assets. It's your absolute, no-nonsense protection. It acknowledges that you think there is at least a one-in-20 chance that economic events will go seriously haywire. If you think the odds are even greater for a severe economic dislocation, then 10% in gold makes sense. Future events may require you to raise this percentage.

The present course of the U.S. government is leading to economic peril. The dismal record of government-run economies leaves little room for optimism. The question is not if we will suffer an economic reckoning, the question is when! When that time comes, gold will be your best friend.

In this century most politicians have believed in a large, dominant role for government. Future centuries may think of the current period as the age of big government. This statism fosters socialism by installments. Some economists have described the mixed economy as a phase in the transition from capitalism to socialism.

As long as this process continues, investors will have no choice but to look at gold as a way to offset losses to their dollar holdings. The dollar loses purchasing power when it declines against foreign currencies. If you own gold, you can't get hurt as much by a devaluation. When the dollar declines, raw materials and products manufactured overseas cost more. A falling dollar may be the chief reason that gold would be good to own. In an environment when all assets plunge in value, gold would likely fall the least. Superimpose any kind of panic or fear on this situation and the price of gold could explode upward.

The dollar acts as the world's reserve currency much as gold once did. If the dollar loses ground and dollar holders suffer losses, they may turn to another currency. A flight from the dollar could overwhelm the monetary authorities. Consequently, gold will likely play a role of growing importance. The worse the fate of the dollar, the more important the role of gold.

It's clear that the dollar is in trouble. In 50 years, over 90% of its purchasing power has disappeared. This trend remains intact and can worsen at any time. Claims that gold will be less important in such an environment simply don't take into account the historical evidence. Whenever paper currencies have inflated away their value, the citizens of the countries involved have turned to gold.

As Ludwig von Mises pointed out, "In many parts of the earth an increasing number of people realize that the United States and most of the other nations are firmly committed to a policy of progressing inflation. They have learned enough from the experience of the recent decades to conclude that on account of these inflationary policies an ounce of gold will one day become more expensive in terms both of the currency of the United States and of their own country. They are alarmed and would like to avoid being victimized by this outcome."

If the nation's $46 trillion of public and private debt were backed by the U.S. gold supply, gold would have to be valued at $300,000 an ounce. The amount of money debt and credit in the United States staggers the mind. The infinitesimally small value of the world's gold supply in comparison to the swollen amount of irredeemable money and credit testify to the abandonment of gold as a factor in monetary affairs. At their peak, the market cap of five big technology stocks exceeds the value of all the gold in the world. By any historical ratio of gold to money (and credit) gold is cheap. Not just inexpensive or undervalued, but dirt cheap.

Will the old ratios of gold to money ever return? Will gold be restored as a monetary metal? I believe the answer is yes. Gold must inevitably become money again. If that were to happen now, those who owned gold would see its value multiply by an unimaginable amount. But it will occur only after an economic crisis or after a series of such disasters. In that case, the value of gold will rise, but the value of everything else will collapse.

Gold acts as a refuge from the effects of government blunders and mismanagement. The yellow metal protects against the ravages of socialism. As economic damage mounts and a crisis looms, gold becomes indispensable. In 1933 gold was confiscated to prop up the dollar and provide international solvency for the U.S. Today the gold held by U.S. citizens would not be nearly enough to accomplish that task. U.S. citizens probably own much less gold today per capita than in the 1930s when gold certificates were a claim on gold. In other words, gold would not be confiscated for the same reason today. Furthermore, the U.S. Mint sells gold coins that it mints for public purchase. It would take extraordinary circumstances to stop gold sales to citizens and take the gold back from those who have already purchased.

A more likely scenario would be the discontinuation of gold sales in the U.S. altogether. A ban on new sales could result from a domestic run from the dollar into gold. In other words, if gold began to compete with the dollar, the government could stop gold sales. That possibility would be more likely than an outright confiscation.

However, if enough gold built up in private hands the equation could change. At that juncture, politicians and bureaucrats might consider seizing gold. They would probably couple this action with public censure of gold holders. Speculators and gold hoarders would make handy scapegoats for those looking to blame a monetary mess on someone other than themselves.

CHAPTER XXXIV

HOW TO AVOID THE PITFALLS AND TRAPS IN GOLD INVESTMENTS

"The market is color blind."
~ W.H. Hutt

Much of the following information comes from the literature of Investment Rarities Incorporated. Here we have reprinted a part of their information on the pitfalls of gold investing. This company provides educational material and economic newsletters that give excellent information on gold and silver. They are also a good source for gold purchases. You can call them toll free at 1-800-328-1860 for literature on precious metals.

They issue this warning: "Although gold has gone up 600% in the past 20 years, some investors in the yellow metal have lost money. We want to show you the traps and pitfalls which triggered these losses and then tell you the exact way a few investors have made big profits in the gold market."

GOLD OR SILVER FUTURES

By putting up a small amount of money, you can hold a futures contract on 100 ounces of gold. Generally you can make money if gold goes up sharply, right after you buy. However, the risks are too high for prudent investors.

If the price of the metal drops, you are required to come up with large sums for margin calls. Heavy trading activity in gold and silver usually means a whopping increase in the maintenance fee you must put up for each contract. This maintenance fee protects the brokerage firm if you fail to meet your margin call. There are also commissions and an interest charge built into the contract.

Some experts believe that 90% of all investors in commodity contracts suffer losses. Big banks, hedge funds and professional speculators play this market, so you are competing against the best. Although commodity futures markets are the chief method of arriving at the daily price for gold and silver, they are generally too risky. Futures contracts are the direct opposite of a conservative gold investment strategy, wherein you take the actual gold into your possession.

LEVERAGE CONTRACTS

If you understand the risks in the futures market, you can clearly understand what's involved in one of the most heavily promoted methods of buying gold or silver – the leverage deal. Several private companies have flourished in the past two decades by offering these investments which are a disguised form of futures contracts.

In a leverage contract, the investor buys a specific amount of gold or silver. A large down payment is required. Carrying costs and commissions are substantial. The metals are supposedly stored in a vault somewhere. In reality, the metals are only indirectly connected to your purchase through a futures contract, which backs up the deal.

In other words, many of the risks in a futures contract are present with a leveraged purchase. Companies who sell these contracts advertise heavily in major financial publications. Often these ads mention coins or bullion and imply that the metals are held in the investor's possession. However, leveraged positions are primarily trading vehicles and promote a short-term philosophy where the investor never sees the coins and bullion.

Furthermore, leverage contracts are more expensive than a futures contract and tend to be quite lucrative for the offering company. The investor would probably be much better off dealing directly in the futures market. Overall risk in leverage transactions seems too high for prudent investors who want to develop a winning long-term strategy.

FINANCED PURCHASES

A number of banks offer partial financing of precious metals and coin purchases. Interest costs and other charges or fees make financing gold a dubious proposition. The gains may not be high enough to absorb the costs and still leave a profit. Precious metals prices have a history of lying dormant for lengthy periods of time and then exploding upward in a short period. If your timing is perfect, you can come out O.K., but most such purchases have turned out to be money losers. Our strong recommendation is to avoid financing your gold purchase.

GOLD AND SILVER OPTIONS

An option means that you have a right to the financial outcome of a futures contract. For an option fee, you can control a certain amount of gold or silver for several months.

Options limit the risk present in a futures contract. They can be profitable in a market moving in one direction. However, whenever the markets heat up, the fee or premium you pay to buy an option increases sharply. If the silver or gold prices don't go up enough to offset this stiff fee, you have lost that amount. However, that's all you can lose.

Commissions on options can be high. For example, if you bought an option on silver for 60 days and the cost was $1,000, as much as $450 of that could be commission. Some firms charge less, but the commission is rarely low.

All the foregoing investments have one thing in common. The buyer never holds the gold in his or her possession. That's contrary to our bedrock advice. You cannot develop a prudent long-term investment strategy unless you get the coins and bullion into your possession.

BULLION STORAGE

This represents a different twist on taking the gold and silver under your control. You turn the physical purchase over to a storage facility and they charge you a fee to keep it there. Some of these storage facilities are first-rate and hundreds of millions of dollars in precious metals sit in their subterranean vaults. Storage fees average 1/2 of 1% of total dollar value of coins or bullion.

However, many storage agreements are between you and the company that sells the metals. They, in turn, have an agreement with the storage facility. Never forget that gold and silver is a feast-or-famine business. Profits are low and dealer mortality high. You never want to store your metal in the name of a company that has problems. If you decide to store your gold, get a storage agreement between you and the storage facility. When you sell, you must sign a release from the bank or vault before your metals are removed.

While we favor taking gold into your possession, we realize there are times when this can be inconvenient. Also when you have much over a half-million dollars of gold in your safe or deposit box, you may need to find another alternative storage place for additional gold. We recommend Brink's as a sensible alternative for large amounts of the yellow metal.

FRAUD

A number of major frauds in the past 20 years have centered around paper transactions and storage programs. To avoid problems, make the following concrete rules:

1. Never let any investment company or dealer hold or store your bullion or coins at their premises or in their name at a storage facility.

2. If you store your metals, make sure the storage plan is directly between you and the storage facility.

3. Never buy metals with a delayed delivery plan or where you are paid a fee to let the dealer use your metal.

4. Never make a down payment and let the dealer hold your coins or bullion. Pay the full amount and take possession.

5. Never fall for purchase plans that offer coins or bullion under the spot price.

6. Never use a purchase plan that allows the dealer to hold the metal and pay you interest on the gold.

7. No matter how large a bank or broker may be they can still fail. Remember Bear Stearns and Lehman Brothers. Consequently

we don't totally trust any counterparty or storage entity other than Brink's. Consequently our advice is to avoid gold exchange traded funds, pool accounts, digital gold, bank storage, brokerage firm storage, foreign storage, blockchains, and storage at mints. A few years ago Morgan Stanley was sued because they refused to provide serial numbers on 1,000-ounce bars of silver they supposedly held for clients. They admitted in court they had no silver stored even though they charged a storage fee. Their defense was "everybody does it."

Most of the frauds in the precious metal business could have been avoided if investors followed these simple rules. Too many investors jump at offers that are too good to be true. Always be leery of outrageous claims coming from brand new firms. A few years ago several scoundrels in Florida advertised they would sell gold at below the spot price. They would then hold the gold for six months before they sent it to you. How could anyone sell gold under the market price or below dealer cost? Investors should have scorned them. Instead they sent them millions to get into this fraudulent offer. The crooks spent the money and never did have the gold. Deal with reputable companies that have been in business for a number of years. If a company offers you something that seems too good to be true you can be sure that it is.

CHAPTER XXXV
GOLD BULLION AND GOLD COINS

"Gold bears the confidence of the world's millions who value it far above the promises of politicians, far above the unbacked paper issued by governments as money substitutes."

~ Oakley R. Bramble

Here are the ways that people own gold in their physical possession:

U.S. Gold Eagle – This is the most popular gold bullion coin in America. These coins are struck by the U.S. Mint. The Eagle is 22-karat and exactly one ounce of gold with ½-ounce, ¼-ounce and ⅒-ounce coins also available. The beautiful Walking Liberty on the Eagle features the famous design by Augustus Saint-Gaudens seen on the older Double Eagle that Teddy Roosevelt initiated in 1907.

American Buffalo – This .9999 gold coin was first minted in 2008. They are beautiful coins featuring the design of the U.S. Buffalo nickel in circulation from 1913 to 1938. Mintage numbers are low.

Canadian Maple Leaf – This 24-karat coin contains one pure ounce of gold. It has a $50 face value. It's produced by the Royal Canadian Mint. It also comes in ½-ounce, ¼-ounce, and ⅒-ounce sizes.

Austrian Philharmonics – This 24-karat gold coin was introduced to gold investors in 1989 by the Austrian Mint, a subsidiary of Austria's central bank. It's one of the world's most popular gold coins. The Philharmonic is minted in four sizes: 1-ounce, ½-ounce, ¼-ounce, and ⅒-ounce. Comparable in price to the U.S. Eagle and the Canadian Maple Leaf, the Philharmonic's high face value of 2,000 Austrian schillings is a popular feature.

Krugerrand – Up until the time it was banned, the South African Krugerrand was the most popular gold coin in the U.S. It's legal again to import Krugerrands. There already are millions of these coins in the U.S. An important component of the gold coin business is in the after-market. Most gold coins trade actively among dealers. The premiums can shrink on the major gold coins if the after-market supply exceeds demand. In the case of the Krugerrand, the premium has virtually disappeared. They trade close to their bullion value.

Mexican 50 Pesos – This big coin weighs in at one-and-two-tenths of an ounce of gold. The Mexican government struck these coins with dies dated in the 1940s so they are called restrikes. Back in the early 70s, before gold was legal, you could own them because the early dates made them legal. These coins have been around since the 70s, but have never caught on in a big way.

Austrian and Hungarian 100 Coronas – These two coins are also both restrikes and contain 98/100 of one ounce of gold. They were extremely popular for a short time in the mid-70s. You can still buy them, but unless the price is quite favorable, we don't know why you would.

Australian Kangaroo Nugget – The Kangaroo Nugget coin is a legal-tender pure gold coin with limited annual mintages. The Kangaroo Nugget is available in five sizes; 1-ounce., ½-ounce, ¼-ounce, ⅒-ounce, and 1/20-ounce.

Foreign Coins – Small foreign gold coins such as the French Rooster, Dutch Guilder, and Swiss Franc, are common bullion coins. They are a good diversification. The biggest problem with these small coins has been price gouging. Certain dealers have sold these coins as rarities and marked them up double or triple over their true value.

Gold "Rounds" – Certain large refineries have minted one ounce gold "rounds" that supposedly compete with bullion coins. However, coin-sized rounds such as the Prospector have never captured much of a following and remain a minor segment of the gold market.

Gold Bullion Bars – Gold bars have never been popular with U.S. investors. Gold coins outsell bars 100 to 1 among the American public. However, for large purchases that go into storage, gold bars may be suitable.

OTHER NEWLY MINTED GOLD COINS

Coins cover a wide spectrum, a few of which are questionable investments. We cover the least appealing first.

Newly-Minted Foreign Coins – Special gold commemoratives from small countries, foreign Olympic coins, Pound, and Sovereign coins all have two things in common: they are pretty and they sell at a wide premium over their gold value. Investors should generally stay away from any collector coins minted in the past ten years. Give these coins a decade or two to season before you consider them.

Another wrinkle aimed at collectors is newly minted sets of medallions put out by private mints. They have no country sponsoring them and are not "coin of the realm." Usually they commemorate certain people, characters or events. They sell at a significant premium over their melt value and should only be purchased for their beauty or collectability rather than as an investment.

COLLECTOR COINS

The desire to collect something old and historical also applies to coins. However, coins have something going for them to which no other collectible can lay claim. Coins have intrinsic value. The gold content merely adds to their value and gives these coins a unique attribute. They can appreciate not only from collector demand, but also from a rise in gold prices.

Many gold buyers worry about the possibility of government confiscation of their gold. They prefer collector coins that have a small premium over their gold value but can be classified as historical or antique collector coins. The U.S. $20 gold pieces fill this particular niche better than any other. You can buy a roll of 20 Double Eagles with at least ten different dates. That gives you a gold coin collection with a variety of mint marks and various dates.

Gold owners like privacy. They don't want the government to know that they own gold. A report to the government is not required at the time you buy gold. However, when you sell coins such as Krugerrands and Canadian Maple Leafs, the dealer must report your sale to the Treasury. Double Eagles, U.S. Eagles, and Austrian Philharmonics, are currently exempt from such reports. The trend in the future will probably be towards more reporting, and because the Double Eagles are not just bullion coins but also collector coins, they have a better chance of staying exempt.

CIRCULATED OR UNCIRCULATED?

The lowest-priced antique U.S. gold coins are circulated. That means that they have some minor wear from passing through various hands after they were placed in circulation. Collectors prefer coins that are uncirculated and pay the highest price for coins that are free of marks, scratches, or blemishes. A rare, high-grade gold coin recently sold for $800,000.

When coins left the mint, they were placed together in bags and almost all such coins have "bag marks," which are small nicks and scrapes. Coins with the least marks bring the best prices. Circulated U.S. gold coins are a low-priced way to own 100- to 150-year-old coins and a preferable alternative to the newly-minted items of today. Antique U.S. gold coins in either circulated or uncirculated condition are the best options.

GRADING

U.S. coins in uncirculated condition are evaluated by a grading system which numbers the coins from Mint State 60 (MS-60) to Mint State 70 (MS-70); the latter being the highest grade a coin can attain. However, MS-70 coins are essentially perfect, and few such coins exist. Most high-grade coins have some minor scratches that may only be visible under magnification. In fact, the perfect coin may not exist.

Coin grading services such as the Professional Coin Grading Service (PCGS) and National Guaranty Corporation (NGC) eliminate most of the grading risk from buying high-priced, high-grade rare gold coins. With lower grades or with circulated coins, this third-party grading is not as necessary.

MS-64 coins are easier to find, and so their price is less than MS-65 coins of the same type. They are extremely attractive coins. MS-63 coins have a few more bag marks but still are attractive and have considerable demand. MS-61 and MS-62 have become popular coins. MS-60 coins are the lowest grade of the uncirculated coins but are more attractively priced. Their bullion content is the biggest factor in their value. They are excellent coins and should be included in most gold coin portfolios.

Circulated gold coins are graded from the well-worn to those that are "almost uncirculated" (AU). Investors should concentrate on the VF grade (very fine), up to the XF grade (extremely fine), and then to the AU grade. These are the highest grades of circulated coins.

19TH AND EARLY 20TH CENTURY U.S. GOLD COINS

Without question, the most popular U.S. gold coins are the Double Eagles. These are $20 gold pieces that contain just under one ounce of gold (.9675).

Liberty Head – This Double Eagle was minted from 1849 to 1907. This 100-year-old coin comes in both circulated and uncirculated condition. Libertys become more difficult to find in MS-64 and MS-65 grades and prices reflect this scarcity. The less expensive XF coins and MS-60 grade coins represent a good gold value for the money.

Saint-Gaudens – Many coin experts claim the Saint-Gaudens to be the most beautiful coin ever minted. The new U.S. Eagle bullion coin copied the design of the Saint-Gaudens. These coins were minted off and on from 1907 to 1933. However, none of the last year were placed in circulation. The lowest priced Saints are several of the more common dates, while the rare 1927D sells for up to $800,000. The Saint-Gaudens is perhaps the premier U.S. coin, and investors should consider it in all grades.

$10 Liberty Head – This mainstay of 19th century U.S. coinage was minted from 1866 to 1907. An earlier and more expensive Coronet style was minted from 1838 to 1866. These coins contain just under ½-ounce of gold. They can be a sound investment in all grades.

$10 Indian Head Type – This beautiful coin shows Liberty crowned with an Indian war bonnet. These coins are more expensive than the $10 Liberty. Although minted from 1907 to 1933, mintages were small.

Minor U.S. Gold Coins – The Liberty Head coins were minted as $5.00 Half Eagles and $2.50 Quarter Eagles. The $2.50 coins were minted in small numbers and are scarce in uncirculated condition. The more common $5.00 coins are a popular investment choice.

In 1908, and for a number of years thereafter, $5.00 and $2.50 Indian Head coins were minted at the various U.S. mints. These unusual coins were struck with an "incuse" design where the Indian and Eagle are sunk into the coin's surface.

Minor U.S. Gold Rarities – The U.S. also struck $1.00 gold coins and $3.00 gold pieces. These coins minted in the middle to late 19th century are found in limited numbers. They sell for high prices that have no relationship to their gold content.

Numismatic Gold – For the advanced collector, a number of numismatic treasures exist. Eagles and Half Eagles were minted as early as 1795. A $4 gold coin, the Stella, is one of the most valuable coins in our history.

Special rarities, like the 1907 Saint-Gaudens struck in high relief, command big prices. Gold commemorative coinage from the early 1900s is highly prized, and the two oversized varieties of the $50 Panama-Pacific coin are worth a small fortune. Numerous gold coins struck in the early West by a variety of private pioneer mints are another highly valuable segment of U.S. gold coin collecting.

CHAPTER XXXVI

GOLD – WHERE DOES IT COME FROM AND WHERE DOES IT GO?

"If you don't own gold, you could be out in the cold."

~ Jesse Cornish

G old is found everywhere in microscopic amounts. The secret is to find a way to extract or mine it profitably. The majority of the gold mined in the world has come from South Africa. South African mines extend deep in the ground and are costly to operate. Although the South African mines are slowly losing production, they still account for over 40% of the world's annual gold mining supply. Simon Black tells us, "In June 1884, a local farmer named Jan Gerritt Bantjes discovered gold on his property in a quiet corner of the South African Republic. Though no one had any idea at the time, Bantjes' farm was located on a vast geological formation known as the Witwatersrand Basin which happens to contain the world's largest known gold reserves.

"Within a few months, other local farmers started discovering gold kicking off a full-fledged gold rush. Just over a decade later, South Africa became the largest gold producer in the world, and the city of Johannesburg grew from absolutely nothing to a thriving boomtown. This area is singlehandedly responsible for 40% of all the gold discovered in human history – some 2 billion ounces (or $2.6 trillion of wealth at today's gold price). And while the Witwatersrand Basin is still being mined to this day, it's not as active as it used to be. Gold production in Witwatersrand peaked in 1970, when miners pulled a whopping 1,000 metric tons of gold out of the ground. A few decades later in 2016, the same area produced just 166 tons – a decline of 83%."

Since the 1980s the United States has offset South Africa's production decline. The U.S. and Canada account for 25% of world production. U.S. gold production is centered in Nevada (60% of the U.S.

total). About 20% of the world's production comes from Russia. No one knows for sure the extent of Russia's gold mining since they have been secretive with production data. In the years ahead, increases in gold production are expected from Mexico, South America, and Asia.

About 90% of the 120,000 metric tons of gold that have ever been mined still exist in the form of bars, coins and jewelry. This may make some gold investors nervous. However, since fully a third of this supply is in jewelry it won't hit the market in quantity. The market only uses about 3,000 tons of gold each year. That means a large above ground supply will always overhang the market. Furthermore, government and private holders are unlikely sellers of massive amounts of gold.

Between 10% and 15% of each year's gold supply comes from scrap. This includes melting old coins and jewelry. Around 90% of the annual supply comes from mining. Of the gold available annually from all sources, three quarters goes into the fabrication of gold jewelry and coinage. Italy remains the world's largest fabricator of gold jewelry, followed by the U.S., India, and Japan. Demand for jewelry continues to grow at a phenomenal rate, and for the long term, the annual supply of gold will likely be fully utilized. The balance goes to private hoarders and industrial users (about 6% of this for electronics). Author Timothy Green discusses this industrial use: "The realization that gold was not just a precious and beautiful metal, but also a versatile and useful one, goes back to the earliest civilizations. Modern technology, however, has found that its traditional virtues of malleability, ductility, reflectivity, and resistance to corrosion, are matched with unparalleled ability as a thermal and electrical conductor. Moreover, once you ally its resistance to corrosion with the facility to convey a tiny electrical current in temperatures varying from -55 to +200 degrees C, then you have one of the foundation stones of modern electronics. I always remember a scientist at Johnson Matthey, the precious metals specialists, saying many years ago, 'When people want something to be 500 percent reliable for twenty years, we recommend gold.' But, mindful of advances in technology, I recently asked an American electronics expert what substitute might be in view. 'Gold is still better than anything else we have evaluated,' he replied. In short, the phrase 'nothing is as good as gold,' often used to advertise jewelry, ought really to be the motto for its industrial and decorative uses. Indeed, bypassing for a moment gold's more traditional applications in decoration and dentistry, one must acknowledge that our present age of high technology finds it indispensable in everything from pocket calculators to computers, telephones to television, and missiles to spacecraft."

Citizens of newly prosperous Asian countries with a history of political or military turmoil are the biggest buyers. In the 1980s, Japan ranked first among buyers, closely followed by Taiwan. They may now be overtaken by mainland China, which continues to be a growing gold buyer. The beneficial inroads of capitalism promise to dramatically increase the ability of the Chinese to purchase gold. Hong Kong and Singapore are also major buyers.

Analyst Alasdair Macleod offers insights into China's enthusiasm for gold: "Not only has China invested in unprofitable gold mines to become the largest producer at about 450 tons annually, but the state monopolizes China's refining capacity. She also imports doré bars for refining from other countries, and without doubt since 1983 has accumulated substantial quantities of bullion. Furthermore, it is the only country that has encouraged its population, through television and other media, to accumulate physical gold. Make no mistake, for the last thirty-three years, the Chinese government has made a credible attempt to gain ultimate control over the physical gold market, and to extend gold's protection to her own citizens.

"This is why, despite American wishful thinking, gold remains at the center of the financial system. It is central partly because China ensures it is, and it is also China's ultimate money for commodity and trade purposes. China most likely has enough gold to fully compensate for her reserve losses from the destruction of the dollar and the other fiat currencies on her reserve book. She is deliberately selling down her dollar exposure anyway, while she can."

Long-term trends indicate a strong demand for gold and a slowly shrinking level of production. This can be offset if high prices bring marginal mines into production. Monetary buying and a lively jewelry market promise to drive up prices. Gold jewelry sales are strong and even a worldwide recession didn't temper demand in Asia.

Gold guru Frank Holmes writes, "Gold is one of the rarest elements in the world. If we took all the gold ever mined and melted it down to a 20.5 meter-sided cube, it would fit snugly within the confines of an Olympic-size swimming pool. Unlike fiat money, of which we can always print more, there's only so much recoverable gold in the world. The only way for us to acquire more is to dig.

"Global gold output has been contracting since 2013. What's more, few new projects and expansions are expected to come online this year, writes Thomson Reuters, 'and those in the near-term pipeline are generally fairly modest in scale.' Indeed, if we look at projects that opened in just the last two or three years, we see that they're of lower grade, meaning they don't produce nearly as much as older, easy-to-mine gold deposits.

"Every year, the pursuit of gold becomes increasingly more challenging – not to mention more expensive – requiring ever more sophisticated tools and technology, including 3D seismic imaging, direction drilling and airborne gravimetry. Compounding the issue is the fact that the number of years between discovery of a new major deposit and production is widening, due to the increase in feasibility assessments, compliance, licenses and more. The average lead time for gold mines worldwide is close to 20 years, though it can sometimes be more, depending on the jurisdiction."

Timothy Green explains the great appeal of gold as jewelry: "The original appeal of gold as it gleamed warmly in the rivers and streams of Africa, Asia, and South America was its beauty. At the dawn of civilization, craftsmen found that it could be worked and fashioned with ease into magnificent ornaments and articles of adornment to enhance the human body. The basic techniques they perfected three and four thousand years ago, of drawing gold into wire to make into delicate filigree or foxtail chains, of casting it into a thousand shapes of flowers, birds and animals, that could also easily be engraved, have changed little. Nor has the basic fact that…gold jewelry remains the premier use of gold. Indeed, the fabrication of karat gold jewelry worldwide has recently exceeded the entire output of the mining industry for the first time. Jewelry is the cornerstone of the gold business. The real difference though, is that what was virtually, until this century, the metal of the privileged and wealthy, is today within the means of millions. Gold jewelry has become a mass market consumer item anywhere from Birmingham (England or Alabama) to Berlin, Bahrain, Bombay, Bangkok, and Beijing. Diamonds, so the catchphrase goes, are forever; gold jewelry is for everyone, everywhere."

Proof that gold is the ultimate hedge against inflation and economic problems can be found in newly prosperous Brazil. This country has severe inflation and currency controls, so demand for gold has soared. Whenever a national currency appears to be shaky and there is some wealth, the citizens rapidly turn to gold.

The wild card in the gold equation is mainland China, where demand for gold began exploding as far back as 1992. Economic growth fosters this growing demand in an area of the world where gold is cherished. If every Chinese were to own one ounce of gold it would take all the world's gold mining production for years to come.

Gold stock broker Blake Joyner once described a trip to Asia: "In Kuching, Sawarak, the Malaysian half of the island of Borneo, I was astonished by what I saw in the street bazaars. Forty or fifty percent of the women were wearing gold – many wore substantial amounts. What is responsible for this increased demand in Kuching? The same as elsewhere in Asia; rising wealth and a strong cultural affinity for gold.

"In Hong Kong, it is impossible to miss the enormous emphasis that Chinese place on gold. Jewelry shops on every block have turbaned Sikhs with shotguns standing guard. Dragons, fish and other animals made of 24-karat gold are everywhere costing $15,000-$30,000, but selling for only 15% above the melt value of the gold. It was difficult to find a Hong Kong woman not wearing gold.

"Even more surprising was my first visit to Canton in 19 years. The rice paddies and vegetable gardens of my memories of 20 years ago, were now apartment buildings and factories. Instead of the ugly Mao jackets of years ago, many young women now wore short dresses and small pieces of gold jewelry. It is estimated that one Cantonese in five bought gold last year. That's one million buyers of gold in one Chinese city! Five million Chinese buy gold each year. With a GNP growing at 10%-15% this year, a savings rate of 38% (the world's highest), and an ancient obsession with gold, tens of millions of Chinese will become new gold owners."

Gold has a big following in the East. That's not likely to change much. Author Lawrence Lepard writes, "Gold represents monetary insurance and in a world that has gone crazy with printed money it will do its job of preserving purchasing power when the irrational belief in government-managed money comes crashing down, as it surely will." Analyst Mark Lundeen agrees. "The day is coming when the world will once again realize why gold and silver are 'precious metals,' because unlike units of currency managed by central banks, gold and silver truly are rare."

CHAPTER XXXVII
WHAT YOU SHOULD DO NOW

"Gold and silver, like other commodities, have an intrinsic value, which is not arbitrary, but is dependent on their scarcity, the quantity of labor bestowed in procuring them, and the value of the capital employment in the mines which produce them."

~ David Ricardo

Remember, the absolute liquidity of gold means it can be turned into cash virtually anywhere in the world. Gold doesn't need a strong financial statement. Annuities and bonds depend on the financial strength of the issuer. The value of gold requires no outside solvency. Gold is recognized and cherished everywhere in the world. No other asset carries such universal recognition and respect.

A high concentration of gold value can be stored in a small place. Gold is easily hidden and highly portable. Gold makes a private high value gift to be given to heirs and passed on to loved ones. In a deflation or asset collapse, gold tends to lose less value than other assets. In the Depression, gold was revalued from $18 to $36 an ounce. In cases of national emergencies, wars, disasters, civil unrest, and financial crisis, gold saves lives, provides comforts, and secures passage.

Gold has the world's longest track record. Four thousand years of evidence proves that nothing else compares. Other assets invariably deteriorate, fail, change, or pass away. Up until this century, gold was the world's money. It was the perfect medium of exchange, unit of account, and store of value. No other asset comes close to meeting the definition of money. Gold protects you like nothing else. If every financial asset that you own goes down the drain you can take your gold out and usually recapture what you put into it. Gold can save your lifestyle.

Once you have made a decision you want to know more about the types of gold available to you and the current prices, I suggest you immediately call Investment Rarities Inc. at 1-800-328-1860. Ask for a broker. That person will answer any questions you might have and make sure you receive our regular newsletter on gold, silver and economics.

Next you should think about how much you want to put into gold and silver. I suggest 10%-20% of your net worth. If things get bad in the economy you may ultimately wish to go higher.

You also need to consider where to keep your gold. A bank safe deposit box will do. (In the 1930s when the banks closed, the safe deposit boxes were still available for entry.) You should also contemplate the purchase of a home safe. This should be built in or hidden in a basement or closet. This makes an excellent place to store your gold.

I leave you with these final thoughts: No major country ever edged further out on a financial limb than the U.S. The gargantuan debt, the leveraging, the trade, and budget deficits, don't represent some new sort of progress or advanced economic strategy. They are as old as mankind, and whenever they have been practiced so wantonly, an enormous price has been paid. We trifle with laws that we don't fully understand. The sorry outcome is as clear to me as it is inevitable.

Henry Hazlitt summed it up nicely. "There are men regarded today as brilliant economists, who deprecate saving and recommend squandering on a national scale as the way of economic salvation; and when anyone points to what the consequences of these policies will be in the long run, they reply flippantly, as might the prodigal son of a warning father: 'In the long run we are all dead.' And such shallow wisecracks pass as devastating epigrams and ripest wisdom. But the tragedy is that, on the contrary, we are already suffering the long-run consequences of the policies of the remote or recent past. Today is already the tomorrow which the bad economist yesterday urged us to ignore. The long-run consequences of some economic policies may become evident in a few months. Others may not become evident for several years. Still others may not become evident for decades. But in every case those long-run consequences are contained in the policy as surely as the hen was in the egg, the flower in the seed."

What we don't know and can't know involves the degree of the coming crunch. A severe decline differs from a total collapse. Suffice to say that something bad must come from all of this economic sinfulness. But also remember that our superstructure of debt along with all the other economic distortions holds the potential to create a black hole of asset destruction. Even those who own a lot of gold will shrink from this dire outcome.

Also, it's worth remembering that most people in this country don't have enough assets to protect themselves from anything truly bad. They can afford but a pittance in precious metals. Furthermore, these people will never believe that they should own gold, no matter what. Therefore, if jobs, government safety nets and retirement assets vanish, most people are finished. In the 1930s the government had the financial clout to mitigate much of the damage. This time it could be different. Such an outcome has the potential to set off an orgy of redistribution and hatred for the affluent.

Finally, if you have read this far you may be in the unique position to be able to buy enough gold to protect yourself and secure your future in an angry and unhappy country. Own your gold quietly, don't confide in friends or relatives who may accidentally disclose this information, and rely on gold before anything else as your insurance against the events predicted in this book. Nothing else will do. Bonds and currencies or other non-tangible assets are not a proxy for gold. Remember that paper is man's money but gold is nature's money.

As some of our predictions begin to unfold, the yellow metal will experience a newfound popularity. The experts in the media, government, and Wall Street will express amazement at the powerful revival of interest in gold. At some point, the monetary authorities may even look to gold to bail them out of the mess that they made with paper money. Quite possibly gold will perform the money function once again. One thing is for sure: gold will make a great comeback.

 **JAMES R. COOK** is the president of Investment Rarities Incorporated in Minneapolis, a company he founded in 1973. Mr. Cook is the author of a best-selling book, *The Start-up Entrepreneur*, and the novel *Full Faith and Credit*. Mr. Cook has received the National Wetlands Conservation Award from the U.S. Fish and Wildlife Service, for preserving and restoring wetlands. He is also the architect of the website neverforget.net, a new way of looking at the horrors of the Holocaust.

INDEX